MARCO POLO

Insider Tips

THAILAND

CHINA
Tropic of Cancer
Hong Kong
MYANMAR
LAOS
VIETNAM
South China Sea
THAILAND
Bangkok
CAMBODIA
Sumatra (Indonesia)
MALAYSIA

www.marco-polo.com

金
行
TAXI

999.9 黃金進口公
漢年房地產公司
敬賀
TAXI

SYMBOLS

 Insider Tip

★ Highlight

 Best of...

Scenic view

Responsible travel: for ecological or fair trade aspects

PRICE CATEGORIES HOTELS

Expensive	over 3,100 baht
Moderate	1,550–3,100 baht
Budget	under 1,550 baht

Prices for a double room. Seasonal surcharges or reductions possible

PRICE CATEGORIES RESTAURANTS

Expensive	over 310 baht
Moderate	155–310 baht
Budget	under 155 baht

Prices for a main course without drinks

 On the cover: Ko Phi Phi – a pearl in crystal clear waters p. 91 | In the jungle around Umphang p. 107

DID YOU KNOW?
Timeline → p. 14
Local specialities → p. 28
Books & films → p. 90
National holidays → p. 113
Budgeting → p. 117
Currency converter → p. 119
Useful phrases Thai → p. 121
Weather → p. 123

MAPS IN THE GUIDEBOOK
(126 A1) Page numbers and coordinates refer to the road atlas
(0) Site/address located off the map
Coordinates are also given for places that are not marked on the road atlas
(U A1) refers to the Bangkok map inside the backcover
(*A–B 2–3*) refers to the removable pull-out map
(*a–b 2–3*) refers to the additional inset map on the pull-out map

INSIDE FRONT COVER:
The best Highlights

INSIDE BACK COVER:
Bangkok city map

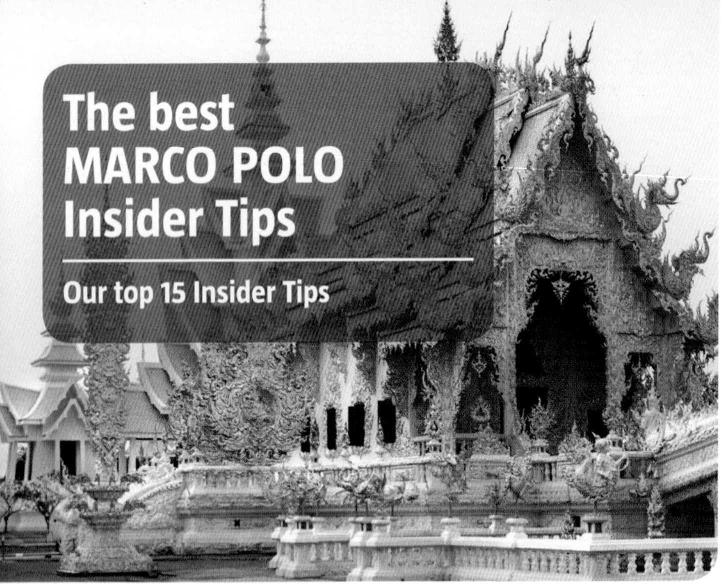

The best MARCO POLO Insider Tips

Our top 15 Insider Tips

INSIDER TIP Tasteful and nostalgic
The *China Inn Cafe* in Phuket Town is a feast for your eyes as well as your taste buds: the city mansion in Sino-Portuguese style is 100 years old, the Thai cuisine is delicious and the fruit yoghurt is decorated with a blue flower → **p. 88**

INSIDER TIP Chill out on the beach
Rustic wooden bungalows surrounded by shady trees, grilled fish under palm leaf roofs and the fire show on the beach: *Porn's Bungalows* on Ko Chang hark back to the days when backpackers had this island to themselves → **p. 69**

INSIDER TIP Pure relaxation
The perfect combination of romance, comfort and a relaxing escape can be found in the paradise that is the *Oriental Kwai* resort near Kanchanaburi. A few days on the river or at the pool, or exploring the area, are just what the doctor ordered! → **p. 42**

INSIDER TIP An artwork in white
Demons, Batman and Buddha -- the *Wat Rong Khun* in Chiang Rai is a whimsical work of art all in white (photo above) → **p. 51**

INSIDER TIP Wilderness adventure
There is no place in Thailand more remote than the Umphang jungle on the Myanmar border. The country's most scenic river, the Mae Klong, is ideal for a boat tour → **p. 107**

INSIDER TIP Oasis of peace
At first glance, Hotel *Rachamankha* in Chiang Mai looks more like a temple furnished with antiques than a guesthouse. It's worth popping in, if only for a drink → **p. 49**

INSIDER TIP Among demons
At the *Sala Kaew Ku* sculpture garden in Nong Khai you have a monumental world of myth and legend almost to yourself → **p. 62**

INSIDER TIP **Stairway to Heaven**

The path is steep: 1,273 steps wind up a mountain from *Wat Tam Sua,* the "temple of the tiger cave", in Krabi. At the top a magnificent panorama awaits → **p. 87**

INSIDER TIP **Dining out with a temple view**

The terrace at *Sala Rattanakosin,* a restaurant near the Grand Palace in Bangkok, provides a stunning view over the Chao Phraya to the Temple of Dawn → **p. 38**

INSIDER TIP **A licence to ride**

In the jungle of the north, earn your elephant riding licence. At *Elephant Special Tours* in Mae Sopok, you can train to be a Mahout → **p. 49**

INSIDER TIP **Luxury bargain**

A luxury hotel suite for only about 70 pounds? It's true – if you're travelling up country. The *Pullman Hotel* in Khon Kaen is the best place to stay in the Northeast → **p. 58**

INSIDER TIP **Eat like the gods**

Delectable dishes from different culinary worlds are served in the trendy restaurant *Mantra* in Pattaya. The food is as heavenly as the name implies → **p. 71**

INSIDER TIP **A piece of China amid in the tea plantations**

Mae Salong in Northern Thailand is home to descendants of the Chinese, who once fled from Mao's army. A cool breeze blows over the coffee and tea plantations (photo below) → **p. 52**

INSIDER TIP **Travel back in time**

History buffs will find just what they are looking for at the *National Museum* in Bang Chiang. Learn all about Thailand's first high civilization from over 3,500 years ago → **p. 63**

INSIDER TIP **Temple of three cultures**

The *Wat Wang Wiwekaram* in Sangklaburi combines Indian, Burmese and Thai styles to create a masterpiece of temple architecture → **p. 43**

BEST OF...

GREAT PLACES FOR FREE
Discover new places and save money

FOR FREE

The nightly enchantment of ruins
No admission is charged for the central area of the *Old Sukhothai* temple on weekdays and Sundays after 6pm. As an added bonus, the lighting makes the place seem all the more mystical at night → p. 45

Traverse a mangrove swamp on foot
Why not save the cost of hiring a longtail boat: in Krabi Town you can walk along the boardwalk of the *Mangrove Forest Walkway* and see nature up close: mudspringers, monitor lizards and crabs → p. 86

Loge seat with a view of the sea
At Cape Promthep on Phuket, hundreds gather every evening to watch the legendary sunsets. The best views are from the *lighthouse,* which doesn't charge an admission fee → p. 88

Temple by the lake
Palm trees on a lily pond and two ornate temples that you can visit for free: *Wat Chong Klang* and *Wat Chong Kham* in Mae Hong Son could easily be the setting for an oriental fairytale (photo) → p. 53

Phra Nang cave phallic shrine
On the neighbouring beaches of Railay in Krabi, there are two exceptional caves – and the more bizarre one is free. In *Phra Nang Cave,* hundreds of wooden phalluses stand surrounding a shrine → p. 86

The view from the summit of the sublime
Most places in Thailand frequented by tourists charge admission to see Buddha. But, you can admire the *Big Buddha* on Phuket at no cost and the spectacular view is free, too! → p. 88

A charming array of temples
As you walk through the historic part of Chiang Mai, you will come across a temple every few minutes that is open to the public for free, including the impressive *Wat Chedi Luang* as well as the *Wat Chiang Man* and the legendary *Wat Phra Singh* → p. 46

Dots in guidebook refer to "Best of..." tips

ONLY IN THAILAND

Unique experiences

Water fight!

If you don't like water, then avoid the Thai New Year festival, *Songkran.* During this "water festival" nobody can escape as revellers soak each other with water pistols, hoses, buckets and bowls. It's all great fun – especially in Chiang Mai in northern Thailand (photo) → p. 112

A house for ghosts

Even the spirits need a home so they don't go out making mischief. So the Thais build little shrines for them, where they leave them offerings. The most famous spirit house in Thailand is the *Erawan Shrine* in Bangkok → p. 22

Transvestite shows

Nowhere else on earth has such flamboyant transvestite shows as Thailand, complete with their troupes of ladyboys *(kratoei).* There costume play is especially spectacularly staged by *Tiffany's Show* in Pattaya → p. 72

Fighting with fists and feet

Thai boxing is an action-packed sport, involving the use not only of fists but also elbows, knees and feet. The excitement in the ring is matched by the atmosphere in the crowd. The best boxers show off their talents at the *New Lumpinee Boxing Stadium* in Bangkok → p. 24

Islands in their thousands

Thailand boasts more islands with gorgeous sandy beaches than anywhere else in Southeast Asia. Whether you're seeking excitement or relaxation, you're bound to find it either in the Gulf of Thailand or the Andaman Sea. A particular unspoiled piece of paradise is *Ko Jum,* where you sometimes encounter more monkeys than tourists on the beach → p. 82

Nights of culinary delights

When night falls, Thailand is aflame! Every night in the cities you hear gas cookers hissing and see charcoal fires glowing. Food stalls at night markets prepare snacks and entire meals, and they're good places to sample regional specialities – such as the grilled locusts at the *night market in Khon Kaen* → p. 57

BEST OF...

AND IF IT RAINS?

Activities to brighten your day

Gather round the wok
How do you make deliciously creamy curry? What gives the shrimp soup, *tom yam gung,* its hot and sour flavours? Discover the secrets of Thai cuisine at a cooking class at the *Blue Elephant* → p. 39

Shopping centres
It's possible to buy just about anything in Bangkok's shopping centres. The city's most important shopping area is along the Skytrain route. From here you have direct and covered access to shopping centres such as the gigantic *Siam Paragon* (photo) → p. 39

Delve into Thailand's history
Explore the history and culture of the country in a light-hearted way at the *Museum of Siam* – thanks to sophisticated technology and a good dose of Thai humour → p. 36

Unbelievable!
It might be hard to believe, but *Ripley's Believe It or Not* in Pattaya has a model of the Titanic made of a million matches and a three-legged horse – as well as 300 other bizarre exhibits → p. 70

Sharks and other fish
Is it possible to walk across the sea with dry feet? Yes, but only at *Sea Life Bangkok Ocean World.* Admire the great variety of ocean inhabitants ranging from terrifying sharks and huge crabs to sweet little penguins → p. 110

A cinema with a touch of luxury
As the rain falls outside, snuggle up in your first-class seat at the *SFX Cinema,* the multiplex facility of the Central Festival in Pattaya. Drinks and snacks are brought right to your seat → p. 71

RELAX AND CHILL OUT

Take it easy and spoil yourself

CHILL OUT

Massage at the monastery

Your feet are sore, your neck is stiff – walking around the city can be tiring. Why not seek refuge at a monastery! Treat yourself to a rejuvenating Thai massage at the *School of massage of Wat Pho* in Bangkok, the perfect remedy for your aching muscles. → **p. 37**

Dinner on the beach

The sound of the sea, sand trickling through your toes, the smell of grilled fish, and torches and fairy lights everywhere: *Chaweng Beach* on Ko Samui is transformed into an open-air restaurant at night. You won't find a more romantic place to dine → **p. 83**

Celestial cocktails

The glass bar glows translucent blue and the city is spread out beneath you as you sip your champagne cocktail. It almost makes you feel you're in seventh heaven. And no wonder: at 220 m (722 ft), the *Sky Bar* in Bangkok has a 360-degree view of the metropolis → **p. 38**

Yoga and meditation

Ko Phangan is renowned for its full moon parties. Yet the island in the Gulf of Thailand is also a place of refuge and a sanctuary for those who wish to learn more about their inner selves. With yoga and meditation you can rediscover body and soul (photo) → **p. 107**

All aboard over the Kwai

Discover life at a slower pace! The leisurely train ride from Kanchanaburi to the sleepy town of Nam Tok follows along the historic tracks of the *Death Railway* over the famous bridge on the River Kwai and a stunning viaduct → **p. 43**

Sundowner on the rocks

The terrace restaurant at the *Rock Sand Resort* on Ko Chang is not much more than a large, rickety shack constructed on an outcrop of rock that provides the foundations. A novel location right on the beach; as you sip your sundowner you can hear the rush of the sea just below → **p. 67**

INTRODUCTION

DISCOVER THAILAND!

A farming village in Northeast Thailand: like a desert island on a vast ocean it stands amidst the paddy fields, which stretch away as far as the eye can see. A monk walks along the dusty village street. An old woman kneels in front of her stilt house and offers the monk her alms: a small plastic bag filled with rice and two hard-boiled eggs. The monk stops and holds out his begging bowl. He does not thank the old woman; it is up to her to give thanks – for having the opportunity to do a good deed. She gets up and climbs the wooden stairs to her house. When she reaches the top, she turns around again. She gazes into the distance, towards where the road loses itself in the rice fields. It leads to Bangkok, the big city. Her son works there as a taxi driver. Caught in the capital's morning rush hour, maybe he's the one who buys the chain of jasmine and orchid blossoms from the hawker – a fragrant good luck charm to be used as a decoration for his rear-view mirror.

Whether you seek solace in a village or are caught up in traffic in Bangkok, one thing is certain: you are in a country like no other. It is a ***land full of secrets***, a strange and exotic place. And yet you won't feel like a stranger for long, for this is also the land of smiles.

Photo: Akha women picking tea on the mountain of Doi Mae Salong

Wat Pho, one of the oldest temples in Bangkok. Thais call their capital city the "City of angels"

It is above all other things the Thai people themselves who have made Thailand the top travel destination in Asia. Granted, it is not always easy to understand them: how, for example, can you fathom a nation which enthusiastically embraces all that is *tansamai* (modern), yet remains highly ***superstitious***? The newest smartphone is an indispensable status symbol for many, while the same individuals are afraid of ghosts and build miniature houses on every corner – or even entire shrines – to appease the spirits.

The spirits weren't always placated in Thailand, however. Although Thais typically seek harmony, preferring restraint to taking up arms, this was not always the case with their neighbours to the northwest: in 1767 the Burmese invaded and annihilated Ayutthaya, one of the most magnificent cities of the age.

8th–11th century Thais migrate from southern China

1238 Sukhothai becomes the capital of the first Thai kingdom

1350 The kingdom of Ayutthaya is established in the south

1512 Portuguese traders arrive in Ayutthaya, followed by the Dutch, English and French

1767 Burmese conquer and destroy Ayutthaya

1782 King Chakri, Rama I, founds the Chakri Dynasty and

When the European powers came to the Far East to divide this part of the world amongst themselves, ***Siam*** was the only country in Southeast Asia that did not fall under colonial rule. As flexible as bamboo bending with the wind to avoid breaking, the nation also strategically manoeuvred itself during the tumultuous years of World War II. Instead of trying to stand up to the far superior forces of the Japanese, they officially became their allies.

The course of Thailand's post-war history was largely decided by generals, who regularly came to power on the back of military coups. Student protests in 1973 and 1976 were brutally crushed. But the ***economic boom*** of the 1980s not only changed Bangkok's skyline, it also had repercussions for its political landscape. The capital in particular saw the emergence of a broad-based middle class, which developed a political consciousness and demanded a say in shaping the nation. While in previous decades it was students who had taken the streets, the dawn of the new millennium gave rise to mass protests. In 2008 government opponents even occupied the international airport in Bangkok. In 2010, supporters of former Prime Minister Thaksin, who had been driven out of office by a military coup, barricaded the main business quarter in Bangkok. The week-long protest was violently brought to an end by the military and the police, and almost a hundred people died in the process. After Thaksin's sister Yingluck won the election that followed in 2011, it was not long before the next military coup in May 2014. Thailand has been governed by General Prayut Chan-o-cha since August 2014.

Most popular holiday destination in Asia – thanks to its people

proclaims the village of Bangkok as the new capital city

1868–1910 King Chulalongkorn, Rama V., sends Thais to be educated in Europe and abolishes slavery

1932 Bloodless coup. Conversion of an absolute monarchy to a constitutional monarchy

1939 Siam is given the name Thailand (Land of the Free)

1946 King Bhumibol Adulyadej is crowned as Rama IX. He is the longest reigning Thai monarch

With an area of 513,120 sq km (198,117 sq mi), Thailand is roughly as large as Spain. Geographically speaking it is divided into ***four regions***. The Central Plains with its fertile alluvial soil is renowned as the rice bowl of the country and, along with the metropolis of Bangkok, is simultaneously one of the most important economic regions. The mountains of the North are the foothills of the Himalayas, where villagers clad in colourful costumes still implement shifting cultivation, and temperatures during winter months are conducive to growing strawberries and apples. The drought-prone Khorat Plateau of the Northeast comprises almost exclusively farmland, despite the mediocre soil. Around 20 million of the total population of 67 million live in this region; otherwise known as the Isan, it is regarded as the poorhouse of the nation, where many villages still have unsurfaced roads and residents get their water from wells or cisterns.

The Central Plains: the rice bowl of the country

Comparatively few tourists travel to the Northeast. And yet in many ways this region is the most authentic part of the country, where the rhythm of life is still determined by sowing and harvesting, by rainy and dry seasons. But who would begrudge a foreigner from a cold climate his preference for a holiday destination where the sea is of a bright turquoise colour and the creamy white beaches make ***holiday dreams*** come true: the South, which extends down to the Malaysian border like the trunk of an elephant. There are fields of pineapple and rows of rubber plantations, coconut palms cast feathery shadows, and fishermen tie colourful scarves and blossom garlands on their boats.

Some of the best dive sites in Southeast Asia

The only Thai city to merit the distinction of "metropolis" is Bangkok. Almost every fourth Thai lives in the commuter belt of the ***gigantic capital***. At first glance, the cosmopolitan city seems like any other modern city with its skyscrapers and bumper-to-bumper traffic. Yet, behind this progressive façade, the traditional Thai lifestyle persists. In the streets surrounded by high-rise residential buildings, popular yet simple dishes are sold from food stalls, motorcycle taxi drivers with their bright yellow vests kid around with each other in the shade of an old tree, and people

1980–88
Thailand's economy booms

1997–98
Economic crisis

2004
A tsunami hits Southern Thailand, devastating communities and killing 5,400 people.

2014
Coup d'etat ousting the government of Yingluck Shinawatra; it is the twelfth successful putsch since the end of the absolute monarchy

2015
A hefty bomb explodes at the Erawan Shrine in the heart of Bangkok, leaving 20 dead and 125 injured in its wake

kneel down and pray to Buddha and Hindu gods before the most modern shopping centres, all reflecting the mix of ***tradition and modernity*** so typical of Thailand. The provincial cities paint quite another picture. Where lovely wooden houses once stood in most places, you will now only find rather ugly, homogeneous concrete buildings resembling stacked boxes. Only every now and then will you come across lovely town centres with old villas and little shops, such as in Phuket Town, Chantaburi or Lampang.

Even up to the World War II most of the kingdom was blanketed by lush greenery: 70 percent of the area was forested. The rapidly growing population, however, has required ever more agricultural land. Today, the forested area has dwindled to approximately 20 percent. There are thought to be only 1,500 wild elephants roam-

Picture-perfect beach: Phra Nang Beach on the coast of Krabi

ing through the jungle, and the number of endangered big cats is estimated in the hundreds. Their sanctuaries make up only a few of the 127 ***national parks*** parks and protected regions, which comprise over half of the remaining forest area in Thailand. Nevertheless, you don't have to go to a zoo to discover Thailand's rich and varied fauna.

The Gulf of Thailand and the Andaman Sea in particular are renowned as having some of the best dive sites in Southeast Asia, though you'll have to be very lucky indeed to see – let alone swim with – a giant plankton-eating whale shark. But every dive school knows where to find the spotted (and harmless) leopard sharks that you can almost reach out and touch. You won't need a guide to enjoy all the brightly coloured coral fish found in these temperate waters. Simply dive down and see!

WHAT'S HOT

1 Flea markets

Totally modern old stuff An increasing number of fashion-conscious Thais are heading to the flea markets to find trendy vintage clothes, furniture and antiques. The best are held in Bangkok where you can stroll along looking for odds and ends as well as a good bargain or two. At the *Chatuchak Weekend Market (photo)* (see p. 39) and the "railway market" *Talad Rod Fai (Sri Nakarin Rd, Soi 51 | eastern side of the city | www.talatrofai.com)*, even those who hate shopping will be delighted by the great variety of items for sale.

2 Sepak Takraw

A ball on the rise Get the kick and the feel the power of Sepak Takraw. This fast-paced mix of volleyball, football and athletics is becoming a national sport in Thailand. It not only involves long passes over a net with the woven ball but also rather artistic overhead kicks come into to play. It's interesting to watch and fun to play. Regular matches of the Thai league take place all over the country (dates listed at *www.sepaktakraw.org)*. The *National Stadium* in Bangkok is one of the sport's most important venues.

3 Progressive

Thai music Indie music is a not a genre that one would necessarily associate with Thailand. However, there is a lively and very popular scene. You can listen to the Thai rock sound both live and as background music in the pubs around Bangkok's Thammasat University, such as the *Phra Nakorn Bar & Gallery (58/2 Soi Damnoen Klang Rd)* or the Good Story *(72–74 Phra Athit Rd)*.

There are lots of new things to discover in Thailand. A few of the most interesting are listed below

Food trucks

4

Everything on wheels The modern version of the beloved street food stall has been put on wheels in converted mini buses or pick-ups. They are jam-packed with everything needed to prepare the drinks and food on offers. Trucks selling American-style juicy burgers are all the rage at the moment in Bangkok. People queue up in front of the trucks belonging to *Daniel Thaiger (usually on Sukhumvit Rd, Soi 38 | www.fb.com/danielthaiger), Mothertrucker (usually near Khao San Rd and at Central World | www.fb.com/mothertruckerbkk) and Orn The Road (usually on Silom Rd and at Central World | www.fb.com/orntheroadbkk)* – they know the food is well worth the wait!

Weekend trips

5

Explore Thailand by plane Since the emergence of discount regional airlines such as *Air Asia (www.airasia.com) (photo), Nok Air (www.nokair.com) or Lion Air (www.lionairthai.com),* flights have become cheaper and more convenient than ever before. Domestic flights hardly cost more than the corresponding coach trip, but they are much faster and give the residents of Bangkok a chance to escape the metropolis - if only for the weekend. As a result, the traditional day trip destinations near the capital are facing stiffer competition from those further away. Not only the tourist hot spots, but also smaller cities such as Nan, Khon Kaen or Loei are attracting an increasing number of Thai tourists on Saturdays and Sundays.

IN A NUTSHELL

AMULETS

All Thais know that misfortune lurks around every corner. That's why they arm themselves with amulets to ward off evil. Amulets are customarily small figures of Buddha or images of famous monks, which Thais hang around their necks, ideally on chains of solid gold. People with particularly hazardous occupations such as bus drivers will garland themselves with as many as a dozen such good luck charms.

Amulets are of course only effective if a monk has blessed them. Although the ritual does not adhere strictly to Buddhism, Thais are not averse to mixing faith with superstition.

BUDDHISM

An estimated 94 percent of Thais are Buddhist. Even today, it is common for young men in rural areas to spend at least a few days, if not weeks or months, in a monastery. In Buddhism, life means hardship. Only those who overcome the cycle of birth and rebirth – and therefore, all suffering – reach Nirvana. One cause of suffering is desire, in particular the desire to possess. Yet the pursuit of affluence has itself become a religion, to which even monks and monasteries have succumbed. Some novices even take money rather than food in their begging bowls, which is something they should not strictly do.

Photo: Haunted houses on Ko Samui

In Thailand, even the Premier can be addressed by his first name. And good manners are appreciated by everyone

ECOLOGY

The environmental protection movement in Thailand is still in its infancy. Ancient buses belch forth their filthy fumes, farmers torch their stubble fields, raw sewage flows into the rivers and seas, and people seem to chuck their litter anywhere they like. Many westerners disdainfully shake their heads, forgetting that things were not so different in their countries, at least until the 1970s.

There is now increasing awareness of the issues in Thailand, and action to match. Entire school classes go out and collect litter from kerbsides, squares and beaches. Diving schools regularly organise underwater clean-ups, and tourists are welcome to help rid coral reefs of old nets, bottles, and other garbage. Hotels advise guests to watch their water consumption, and air conditioners automatically switch off when guest leave their rooms. There are now initiatives to increase the use of cloth instead of plastic. Each tourist can make a contribution to this end by foregoing plastic bags while shopping.

FARANG

Thais refer to all white-skinned foreigners as farang – which is not a derogatory term. It simply means "white stranger" and is likely a malapropism of the English word, foreigner. And by the way, it also means "guava fruit".

Buddha is omnipresent in Chiang Mai, a city with over 300 temples

HAUNTED HOUSES

Even though they might be devout Buddhists, the world of the Thais is full of *phii*, spirits. The spirits must have their own house to stop them from wandering about and creating mischief. Whether the house is the size of a birdhouse, or is as grand and opulent as a temple, is immaterial. The invisible neighbours are always pleased with the gifts bestowed on them by mortals: flowers, rice, a glass of water, and on important days, a fried chicken.

The ● *Erawan Shrine* on the corner of Ploenchit Rd/Ratchadamri Rd in Bangkok is famous throughout Thailand: here, dancers in ornate costumes express their reverence to the spirits. The shrine is dedicated to the Hindu god, Brahma. When the Erawan Hotel (now called the Grand Hyatt Erawan) was being built in the 1950s, there was a spate of fatal accidents. In order to appease the spirits dwelling in the structure, a shrine was built. From that day on, no more workers were killed. Unfortunately, the Erawan Shrine also made international headlines in August 2015 when a bomb exploded, killing 20 people and injuring 125 others.

HILL TRIBES

The *chao kao,* the people of the mountains, are commonly referred to as hill tribes, a term used in Thailand for all of the various tribal peoples who migrated from southern China and Tibet over the past few centuries. They are an estimated 800,00 people. The largest tribe comprising around 320,000 members are the Karen, who mostly settled along the entire border between Thailand and Myanmar.

The authorities have curbed the cultivation of poppies for the manufacture of opium and heroin, and numerous internationally backed projects have been promoting the cultivation of vegetables, fruit, coffee and tea in the mountains. Trekking tourism has provided many villages with an additional source of income.

KINGDOM

Although Thailand has not been an absolute monarchy since 1932, the royal family is held in high esteem. Insulting the monarch has always been a criminal offence.

The head of the Chakri Dynasty, King Bhumibol Adulyadej, known as Rama IX, is revered at all levels of society. The monarch, born in America in 1927, came to the throne in 1946 and has maintained and even increased his authority as sovereign lord amid all the political turmoil of recent years. He and Queen Sirikit have four children: Princess Ubol Ratana (born in 1951), Prince Maha Vajiralongkorn (1952), Princess Maha Chakri Sirindhorn (1955) and Princess Chulabhorn Walailak (1957).

MANNERS

Thais are tolerant and don't meddle in other people's affairs. However, there are situations where tolerance reaches its limits, such as when derogatory remarks are made about the royal family.

Buddhism, its followers and symbols must be treated with respect. Shoes must be removed in temples (not applicable to Chinese temples), mosques and private residences. Women are not allowed to touch monks, and are also not permitted to sit beside them on buses.

Not paying attention to your appearance means you lose face. Temple visits or appointments with authorities require appropriate attire. Failing to adhere to the strict dress code may result in being denied admission or poorly served – or not served at all. Topless bathing is a violation against local customs. Anyone who displays anger openly is similarly reviled: for Thais, the loss of self-control is one of the worst human characteristics.

The head is not regarded as "sacred", as some Westerners think, but figuratively, as well as literally, it is the highest part of the body. A foreigner should not touch a local's head, even if it is meant in a friendly way. The soles of the feet are the lowest part of the body, and must not be shown to anyone.

NAMES

Whether a postman or a prime minister: Thais generally address each other by first name, preceded by the title *Khun* (man or woman). It is rare to find a Thai person who has no nickname (*chuu len*, literally: "playname"). Animal names are very popular. Westerners might be taken aback when somebody nonchalantly introduces himself as *mu* (pig), *kob* (frog), *gung* (crab) or *gai* (chicken). The unofficial second names are already bestowed on infants by their mothers.

POPULATION

Thailand has a population of about 67 million. Thais are the main ethnic group, comprising 75 percent of the total. 14 percent have Chinese ancestry. Muslim Malays (an ethnic group, as opposed to a nationality) make up 4.9 percent of the population and live in the provinces near the Malaysian border. The remaining population is made up of ethnic Khmer, Laotian, Vietnamese, Mon and Shan, as well as various tribal peoples.

PICK-UP TRUCKS

Thailand is not only the land of smiles, but also the land of pick-up trucks. Just take a look at the traffic outside the capital of Bangkok and you will see the evidence straight away. Just as many pick-up trucks as normal cars are registered every year and not just because the state charges a lower tax on them compared to normal automobiles. These utility vehicles with their large, open beds embody the easy-going and fun side of the Thai lifestyle, and they also come in handy as a large taxi for family trips at the weekend, as a place to sit and drink a beer (or whisky) at the end of the day, or as a way to transport rice, fruit and whatever else.

PROSTITUTION

The Prevention and Suppression of Prostitution Act of 1996 aims to curtail the sexual abuse of minors in particular. Clients of those under 18 years of age face up to three years in prison or six years if the child is under age 15. Stiffer sentences of up to 20 years apply to procurers, seducers and traffickers of children. Lesser punishments apply to the prostitution of adults, which is in fact prohibited if it is "openly and shamelessly" offered.

The number of female, male and transsexual prostitutes is estimated between 200,000 and 800,000. The tourist industry has contributed greatly to the spread of prostitution and the sexual exploitation of children in particular. Since 2003 residents of the UK and the USA may also be prosecuted at home.

SPELLING

Are you, white stranger, a *falang* or a *farang*? Are you on holiday in Ko Samui or Koh Samui? *Ko(h)* means island, but why are there two ways to spell it? Why is a beach sometimes *hat*, in other instances had and sometimes written as *haad*? Newcomers always ask about the vagaries of the language, but rarely get a straight answer. To foreigners, the Thai script is akin to a book with seven seals, written in graceful yet unintelligible squiggles. And there is no hard-and-fast rule for transcribing these lines into Latin characters.

THAI BOXING

The national sport *Muay Thai* uses gloved fists, but also the feet. To heighten the excitement matches are accompanied by drums, and the atmosphere in the stands is almost as exciting as the fight in the ring. Notorious gamblers, Thais never pass up the chance of a bet, especially during a fight. Matches are organised in all provincial cities, but the best fighters step into the ring in Bangkok. Watch the action at ● *New Lumpinee Boxing Stadium (Ram Inthra Rd | www.muaythailumpinee.net)* on Tuesdays, Fridays and Saturdays.

TRANSVESTITES

Women who used to be men (or are still men beneath their clothes) are a common sight in Thailand. Particularly pretty *kratoei*, or ladyboys, appear in transvestite shows at the main tourist centres. Many observers are astonished that such seductive creatures on the stage are not actual women, and that even an attractive bosom does not guarantee that the individual is one hundred percent female. Many transvestites are also prostitutes, but many have regular jobs, which is common in Thailand. Thais enjoy poking fun at the ladyboys, though it's all meant in good humour.

Kicking allowed: fighters also use their feet in Thai boxing

WAI

Thais don't greet each other with a handshake but with a *wai*. In this graceful gesture, both hands, palm to palm and fingers together, are raised towards the face in a prayer-like fashion. This sounds much simpler than it really is, since there are various rules to observe. For example, the youngest person greets first, and so does an individual of lower rank. Thais will look amusedly at your attempt to mimic the greeting. It is completely acceptable to simply greet with a friendly smile and nod of the head. Never reciprocate a child's, servant or beggar's wai – you will look ridiculous.

WALKING STREETS

For a few years now, markets set up on specific days along streets that have been closed down for them have been quite popular. The array of items for sale varies greatly. Whereas plenty of snacks and rummage goods plus cheap plastic toys are sold on the provincial markets in places like Lampang, the Sunday Walking-Street in Chiang Mai and, with some exceptions, the daily street markets in Mae Hong Son and Pai are veritable treasure troves for creative yet inexpensive souvenirs. One of the main traffic arteries in Bangkok, Silom Road, is also closed on Sundays to make room for market stalls and food trucks.

WAT

Wat is the term for a temple, but it can also refer to the entire monastery compound. An exception is *Wat Phra Kaeo* in the Grand Palace in Bangkok: this temple has no monastery attached. The prayer hall of a Wat is called a *bot;* the *chedi* (stupa) is a bell-like tower; a classic Khmer-style stupa is known as a *prang*.

FOOD & DRINK

Thai food is not only considered among the best in the world, it is also exceptionally healthy. It is inimitable and distinctive, yet influenced especially by Chinese, Indian and Malaysian cuisine.

Eateries steam and sizzle on every corner. Street vendors sell grilled squid, kebabs, and ice-chilled fruit. Mobile ***food stalls*** set up at the roadside, a few chairs and a table occupy the pavement, the open-air restaurant is ready for business.

Whether done over a hissing gas stove or charcoal, the food will be delicious: noodle soup with chicken or duck, fried rice with crab, an omelette with mussels or pancakes with pineapple. Meat is used in abundance; poultry and seafood are also likely to be a part of the meal. Vegetables are cooked al dente to retain their vitamins. Various spices and herbs such as coriander, lemongrass and lemon leaves, Thai ginger and basil, tamarind, mint, curry and shrimp paste give Thai food its signature zest. And don't forget the garlic and chillies!

Only upmarket restaurants keep to strict mealtimes such as lunch (around 11:30am–2pm) and dinner (around 6–10pm). Most establishments will carry on serving until late at night and hot food stalls in the larger cities and tourist centres are open virtually around the clock. If not otherwise stated, all restaurants mentioned in this guide are open daily.

Photo: *Tom yam gung*, a classic Thai dish

Thai cuisine is often spicy, yet always light – and for dessert, a heavenly selection of fruit awaits

Thai dishes are served in bite-sized portions or are easily cut with a spoon and fork. Held in the right hand, the spoon is used for eating, while the fork serves only to slide the food onto the spoon. Only noodle dishes and soups are eaten with chopsticks, which have been inherited from the Chinese. A ***typical Thai meal*** to go round a group consists of up to five flavours: bitter, sweet, sour, salty and hot. Meals are served with a big bowl of rice. Dishes can be eaten in any order and everyone just tucks in. Usually, only one dish (with rice) is put on the plate at the start of the meal. Only when it is finished comes the next dish for you to taste. This way, the different tastes don't mix on the plate.

Thais use generous amounts of ***chilli***, though in tourist restaurants they tend to be used more sparingly. To err on the side of caution, you can state your preference for *mai peht* (not spicy). Guests can season standard dishes such as fried rice, fried noodles or noodle soup

LOCAL SPECIALITIES

gaeng kiau wan gai – green curry with chicken and aubergine, slightly sweet *(wan)*

gaeng massaman – red curry with strips of beef, peanuts and potatoes (mildly hot), especially popular in Southern Thailand (photo left)

gung hom pa – battered shrimp, especially tasty when dipped in tartare sauce or a sweet and sour vinegar sauce with sliced chilli

kao niau – sticky rice, a favourite in Northeastern Thailand to accompany spicy salads

kao pat – fried rice with egg *(kai)* and vegetables *(pak)*. Other ingredients are crab *(gung)*, pork *(mu)* or chicken *(gai)*

kuai tiao nam – noodle soup, originally a Chinese import; usually made with pork or chicken, but especially tasty with duck *(pet)*. Thailand's favourite snack (photo right)

nam tok – a spicy salad with strips of beef (nuä) or pork and plenty of fresh herbs mixed with ground roasted rice

plamuk tohd katiam pik thai – strips of squid, fried with garlic and pepper (not hot)

som tam – salad made of thin strips of green papaya, with cocktail tomatoes, dried shrimp, fish sauce and lots of chillies. Raw vegetables, sticky rice and grilled chicken *(gaiyang)* go well with this dish

tom kha gai – soup made with chicken and coconut milk, a particularly exotic treat. Caution: although the broth is not as spicy as in other soups, it still contains chilli peppers!

tom yam gung – sour shrimp soup with lemongrass and lots of chillies. Thailand's unofficial national dish

yam wunsen – glass noodle salad with herbs, shrimp and ground pork. Caution: chillies give this salad its bite!

themselves: each table has its own small container with dried and ground chilli peppers, sugar (for the noodle soup) as well as a sweet-and-sour vinegar containing pieces of chilli. ***Nam pla***, a light brown liquid made from fermented fish is used instead of salt. When substituted with chopped chillies, it's known as *pik nam pla* – don't use too much!

Salads are not like Western-style salads. A typical ***Thai salad (yam)*** is more like a main dish and is eaten as a snack. And it is nearly always very spicy! The hearty *yam nua,* for example, is a slightly sour tasting salad with stir-fried beef strips, garnished with garlic, coriander, onion and crushed chilli peppers. Another popular dish is *yam wun sen,* which features glass noodles as its main ingredient.

Thais love their ***sweets*** *(kanom),* sweet being the operative word. The small calorie-rich desserts are found in every colour of the rainbow at food stands at festivals, on markets and from street vendors. Especially popular are the delicious treats made of sticky rice wrapped in banana leaves and cooked in coconut milk.

Thailand is an oasis for ***exotic fruit***. To Thais, the durian (famous for its odour) is the "king of fruits". The pale yellow flesh under its thorny husk is almost like custard; you're either addicted straight away or put off forever. The mango *(mamuang)* goes especially well with concentrated coconut milk and sticky rice. Thais also adore green mango strips, which they dip into a mixture of sugar and chillies. Beneath the wine-red peel of the mangosteen *(mangkut)* lies a delicate white, juicy fruit that has both a sweet and somewhat sour taste. Also try the hairy rambutan*(ngo),* the fine lychees *(lintshi)* or the bell-shaped red Java apples *(djompu)*.

Dining under palm trees is on everyone's agenda in Thailand

The selection of freshly-squeezed fruit juices on markets is also very varied. Bottled drinking water *(nam bau)* and mineral water is available everywhere. The most popular local beer is *Chang*. Other beer brands brewed in Thailand are Heineken, Tiger, and Singha. The inexpensive rums, *Mekhong* and *Saeng Som,* are distilled from sugar cane and marketed as "whisky". They are not served neat but as a long drink with soda water, and a generous splash of lime juice. Tourists often enjoy this beverage mixed with Sprite or cola.

SHOPPING

Thailand has an astonishing range of products to entice the shopper. Typical souvenirs such as hand-painted paper umbrellas, lacquerware or carved elephants are not all there is on offer. Items such as shoes, brand name drugs, spices and clothing are often available at a fraction of the cost that you would pay back home. Department stores have fixed prices, and many individual shops display their prices too, but it is still possible to negotiate. Haggling with street vendors is compulsory and it can also be lots of fun if you enjoy the banter and jokes that go along with it.

ANTIQUES

Antiques require an export licence, and a reputable business will organise this for you; the body responsible for licences is the *Department of Fine Arts (tel. 0 22 21 78 11)* in Bangkok. However, genuine Thai antiques are rare, so dealers will often stock items originating from many Asian countries, such as Chinese porcelain or historical maps from colonial times. Caution: an entire industry in Thailand has been built on passing off new wares as antiques.

BUDDHA STATUES

Even brand new Buddha statues cannot be exported without a licence. A reputable dealer will acquire the licence on your behalf. The export of historical Buddha figures is generally prohibited.

COSMETICS

Follow your nose! Cosmetics are usually located on the ground floor in department stores, often occupying the entire floor space. Thai women adore perfumes, creams, etc, and the choice of products is correspondingly huge.

CUSTOM-MADE CLOTHING

Arrange at least one fitting with the tailor and don't be afraid of requesting alterations, if necessary. A deposit is usually required, but make sure you're completely satisfied with your garment before paying the balance.

FASHION & ACCESSORIES

In Thailand you can find brand-name fashion from all over the world, as well

Whether you're looking for pearls or perfume, made-to measure clothing or stylish accessories: Thailand makes shopping fun

as shoes and accessories from well-known labels. But local designers are increasingly creating a stir with their creations. Bangkok is by far the best shopping destination for fashion chic: in the enormous shopping centres and department stores, shopping sprees are difficult to resist.

GOLD & JEWELLERY

Never buy jewellery from a street vendor; and don't let yourself be lured into shops by pushy touts! Gemstone scammers, who work with dubious jewellers, lie in wait for naive tourists near the main attractions in Bangkok in particular. Gold jewellery up to 23 Karat is available in special gold shops, which you will recognise by their red interior. Prices are based on the current gold price plus approx. 10 percent for processing.

PEARLS

Thailand's cultivated pearls come from the waters off the island of Phuket in the South. It's possible to visit farms to learn about the seeding process and how the precious gems grow in their oyster shells.

PIRATE COPIES

Pirate copies are available for brand names and anything that is costly, such as watches, T-shirts, jeans or perfume. You will have no trouble with the Thai police purchasing such items, but it may be a different story with customs officials when you get home.

SILK

Since traditional Thai silk is hand woven, each silk fabric is unique. It is never completely smooth, having a slightly coarse feel that makes it warm and vibrant to touch but doesn't diminish its elegance.

CENTRAL THAILAND

The water of the Chao Phraya and its tributaries has made the alluvial plain north of Bangkok the most important rice-growing region in the country. The paddies, where succulent green shoots spring up at the beginning of the rainy season, stretch towards the horizon.

Sukhothai marks the beginning of northern Thailand. It is also where, in 1238, the Thai nation was born with the founding of the first city. Seeing the Historical Park through the dew-laden morning light, and how the rising sun casts its delicate sheen over Buddha statues and columns, chedis and prangs, you can easily see why this place was called the "Dawn of happiness". Yet it's a happiness that did not last for long: Old Sukhothai is now in ruins, a monument in stone to a glorious past. Ayutthaya, the second royal city, also had to learn from Buddha's teachings: "Nothing is permanent". However, while Sukhothai was abandoned and fell into decay, Ayutthaya was destroyed by the Burmese in 1767.

The capital Bangkok is a world metropolis. Only two hours to the west, however, in the province of Kanchanaburi, an entirely different landscape awaits: past the fields and wasteland, jungle-covered hills and mountains suddenly appear. Close to the border of Myanmar the land is raw, wild and only sparsely inhabited. Nevertheless, here you can visit another chapter of history: the world-famous Bridge over the River Kwai and the "Death Railway" are enduring reminders of the horrors of World War II.

 Photo: Wat Phra Kaeo at the Grand Palace in Bangkok

Ancient royal cities and a world metropolis: from the Cradle of Siam via Bangkok to the wild frontier of the Three Pagoda Pass

AYUTTHAYA

(131 D5) *(🕮 D8)* **The rivers of Chao Phraya, Pasak and Lopburi flow around the historic core of the city of 60,000 inhabitants ★ Ayutthaya. Thus the most important sights are found on an island 3 km (2 miles) long and 1.5 km (1 mile) wide.**

The historical centre is peppered with temple ruins and palaces whose columns and towers still define the skyline. Located 76 km (48 miles) north of Bangkok, Ayutthaya is visited mostly by day trippers. There are convenient connections from Bangkok by bus *(every 20–30 minutes from Mo Chit bus station | Skytrain/subway: Mo Chit Station | 50–65 baht)*, by train *(hourly)*, and minibuses from Victory Monument *(Skytrain station Victory Monument | 60 baht)*. Organised bus tours cost approx. 790 baht.There are also combined bus/boat tours (approx. 1,770 baht) with the boat going as far as Bang Pa In.

SIGHTSEEING

ANCIENT PALACE

This is where the kings resided, close to the north-western section of the city wall. As with Bangkok's Grand Palace, a royal temple *(Wat Phra Si Sanphet)* stands in the palace grounds; its three massive, restored chedis are Ayutthaya's landmark. *Daily 7am–6pm | admission 50 baht*

Deeply rooted: Buddha head at Wat Mahatat in Ayutthaya

AYUTTHAYA HISTORICAL STUDY CENTER

A striking exhibition devoted to the city's history and the lives of its kings and subjects. *Tue–Sat 8:30am–4:30pm | admission 100 baht | Rotchana Rd | south of Phraram Park*

BAAN HOLLANDA

The Europeans and Japanese settled in the district to the southeast of the historic centre that is now home to an interesting and modern exhibition on the history of the Dutch settlement in multicultural Axutthaya. *Daily 9am–5pm | admission 50 baht | Soi Ksan Rua | south of Wat Phanan Choeng | www.baanhollanda.org*

CHANDRA KASEM PALACE

This palace was among the buildings destroyed by the Burmese in 1767, but it was restored under the rule of King Mongkut in the 19th century and used as a royal residence. Objects from the royal collection are on display here. Near the palace stands a four-storey tower, the *Phisai Salak,* from where the monarch, a keen astronomer, observed the stars. *Wed–Sun 8:30am–4pm | admission 100 baht*

WAT MAHATAT

This enormous temple complex located on the eastern edge of Phraram Park in the old city centre *(daily 8am–6pm | admission 50 baht)* is perhaps Ayutthaya's most striking monument. As you walk around the perimeter wall, don't miss the iconic image of the severed Buddha head cradled in the roots of a banyan tree. At night, the complex is even more majestic under the floodlights.

FOOD & DRINK

Try the fare at the food stands at the night market Hua Ra by the river opposite the Chankasem Palace or the stands in Phraram Park. For a tasty but cheap noodle soup, head northeast of Wat Mahathat to *Ang Lek Noodle (Chikun Rd),* which is always busy at lunchtime.

WHERE TO STAY

BAAN TEBPITAK

Friendly, family-run guesthouse with comfortable rooms and a pool. *10 rooms | 15/19 Pathon Rd, Soi 3 | mobile tel. 08 98 49 98 17 | www.baantebpitak.com | Budget–Moderate*

KANTARY HOTEL

The best hotel on the square offers spacious rooms with all the amenities at a good price and a pool. *174 rooms | Rojana Rd | tel. 0 35 33 71 77 | www.kantarycollection.com | Moderate–Expensive*

INFORMATION

TOURISM AUTHORITY OF THAILAND

Si Sanphet Rd | tel. 0 35 24 60 76

WHERE TO GO

BANG PA IN (131 D5) *(🕮 D8)*

The royal summer palace with its enchanting, classic Thai-style water pavilion, *Aisawan Thippaya-art,* is situated on an island in the Chao Phraya, 18 km (11 miles) south of Ayutthaya. As in the Grand Palace in Bangkok. visitors should make sure to wear appropriate clothing. Minibuses leave from the Chao Prom Market when there are enough passengers for the tour to the Bang Pa In. *Daily 8:30am–4:30pm| admission 100 baht*

BANGKOK

MAP INSIDE THE BACK COVER (131 D5–6) *(🕮 D9)* **Although the international usage "Bangkok" has prevailed, Thais prefer to call their capital city (pop. approx. 9 million) by its more beautiful name: Krungthep, "City of Angels".**

The best way to get around the city quickly and cheaply is either by the elevated *Skytrain.* An underground metro line operates between the central station via Silom Road and Sukhumvit Road and the Chatuchak Weekend Market. For

MARCO POLO HIGHLIGHTS

★ Ayutthaya
In the old royal city on the trail of the "Golden Age": ruins recall ancient splendour and greatness → p. 33

★ Grand Palace and Wat Phra Kaeo
You absolutely must visit this majestic complex in old Bangkok and admire the unique whimsical architecture → p. 36

★ Chatuchak Weekend Market
Go bargain hunting at this superlative flea market in Bangkok: find whatever your heart desires at one of over 10,000 stands → p. 39

★ Sangklaburi
An adventure to the Three Pagodas Pass in the wild frontier → p. 42

★ Death Railway
A journey along the infamous stretch of track, from the world-famous bridge on the Kwai to the end station, Nam Tok → p. 43

★ Old-Sukhothai
Travel back in time to the birth of a nation: Sukhothai was the first Thai capital city. Today, the graceful ruins are reminiscent of the "Dawn of happiness" → p. 44

more detailed information about the capital, consult the MARCO POLO guide "Bangkok".

SIGHTSEEING

GRAND PALACE AND WAT PHRA KAEO ★ (U A3–4) (*a3–4*)

The *royal palace,* with its *Temple of the Emerald Buddha (Wat Phra Kaeo),* is the most famous historic site in Thailand. Behind their whitewashed walls, the various structures, crowned by intricate roof details and shiny golden spires, have a magical appeal. Demons and mythical creatures watch over the complex, while splendid murals recall life in the royal court and the life of Buddha. The Emerald Buddha in the Royal temple is actually made of jadeite rather than emerald, and is only 66 cm high, yet it is regarded as a national shrine. Tourists can only get in wearing appropriate attire; short or very loose trousers, miniskirts, leggings, shoulder-free tops and open sandals are frowned upon. Appropriate clothing can be borrowed for a fee. Admission also entitles you to visit the *Royal Decorations and Coin Pavilion (in the palace grounds), the Ananta Samakhom* throne hall (U C2) (*c2*) and *Vimanmek Royal Palace* (U C1) (*c1*), the largest teak wood palace in the world. *Daily 8:30am–4pm | admission 500 baht | Na Phralan Rd | www.palaces.thai.net*

CITY WHERE TO START?
Sanam Luang (U A3) (*a3*):
The large open space is a perfect starting point for exploring the historical city centre. The Grand Palace, Wat Pho and Museum of Siam are only a few steps away, and the Old Town area of Banglamphoo with its travellers' hangout, Khao San Rd, are within five minutes' walk. The Sanam Luang (royal square) is served by bus routes 25, 507 and 508. Nearest metro station: Hua Lamphong; Skytrain: National Stadium.

KLONG (U A–B 4–6) (*a–b 4–6*)

In the district of Thonburi, both people and goods are still transported on the *klongs* (canals). You can book a tour at any travel agency, or charter a long-tailed motorboat with driver. Boats are available on the Chao Phraya river (behind the Grand Palace at the Tha Chang pier or at the Sathon pier near the Saphan Taksin Skytrain station). *Approx. 1000–1,200 baht per hour (negotiable!)*

INSIDER TIP MUSEUM OF SIAM ● (U A4) (*a4*)

The museum provides visitors with an excellent and modern introduction to Thailand's dynamic history and culture. The fun multimedia exhibits tell the story of

Race over the streets of Bangkok with the skytrain – an easy way to get from place to place

Thailand from the emergence of Siam to the present day. *Tue–Sun 10am–6pm | admission 300 baht, after 4pm free | Sanamchai Rd | www.museumsiam.com*

JIM THOMPSON HOUSE (U D3) (*d3*)

American Jim Thompson rebuilt the Thai silk industry after World War II. Asian art objects and antiquities of exquisite beauty can be viewed at his former residence. *Daily 9am–6pm | admission 100 baht | Rama I. Rd, Soi Kasemsan 2 | www.jimthompsonhouse.com*

WAT ARUN (U A4) (*a4*)

The "Temple of the Dawn" is one of Bangkok's main landmarks. Looking particularly prominent from across the river, its 67-m (220-ft) high central prang is richly decorated with porcelain and coloured glass. *Daily 8am–5pm | admission 50 baht | in Thonburi | boats depart regularly from Tha Thien Pier near Wat Pho over the river | www.watarun.net*

WAT PHO (U A4) (*a4*)

The oldest university of the country was founded in 1789 in this temple south of the Grand Palace. The complex accommodates a 46-m (151-ft) long gilded reclining Buddha with mother of pearl inlays on the soles of its feet. Take a course at the monastery's *massage school (tel. 0 26 22 35 51 | www.watphomassage.com)*, the most famous in Thailand, and get a massage (from 420 baht per hour). *Daily 8am–6:30pm | admission 100 baht | Entrances on Chetuphun and Thai Wang Rd | www.watpho.com*

FOOD & DRINK

CABBAGES & CONDOMS (U F5) (*f5*)

Delectable Thai meals are served either outdoors in a garden or in the air-conditioned restaurant. The restaurant belongs to an organisation for birth control and AIDS prevention, and the décor features attention-grabbing fantasy creatures covered with coloured condoms. Even the bill includes a condom. *10*

Sukhumvit Rd, Soi 12 | tel. 0 22 29 46 11 | www.cabbagesandcondoms.com | Moderate–Expensive

INSIDER TIP SALA RATTANAKOSIN (U B3) (*b3*)

This elegant restaurant near the Grand Palace serves delightful western-style and Thai dishes. The patio with a view of the river and the Wat Arun when it is lit up at night is very romantic. *39 Maharat Rd | alley behind Wat Pho | tel. 0 26 22 13 88 | www.salaresorts.com* | Expensive

INSIDER TIP SEVEN SPOONS (U B3) (*b3*)

A chic, but restrained atmosphere combined with friendly and competent service plus excellent, Mediterranean-inspired cuisine with an Asian flair at very reasonable prices. The cocktails are tasty, too. *22–24 Chakkrapatipong Rd | tel. 0 26 29 92 14 | www.sevenspoonsbkk.com* | Moderate–Expensive

SIROCCO (U C6) (*c6*)

Savour Western-Mediterranean cuisine at one of the highest open air restaurants in the world (220 m/722 ft) – a culinary as well as an optical pinnacle. Afterwards, enjoy a heavenly cocktail at the ● *Sky Bar. State Tower | 1055 Silom Rd | tel. 0 26 24 95 55 | www.lebua.com/sirocco* | Expensive

SHOPPING

The main shopping streets are *Sukhumvit Rd* (U F4–5) (*f4–5*), *Silom Rd* (U C–D 5–6) (*c–d 5–6*), *Ploenchit* (U E4) (*e4*) and first and foremost, *Rama I Rd* (U D–E4) (*d–e4*) around Siam Skytrain station. There you'll find gigantic shopping centres as well as boutiques and street merchants. A quite unique area with special shops and plenty of hustle and bustle is Chinatown - walk down *Sampeng Lane* (U B4) (*b4*) at any time of day.

Literally everything can be found on Chatuchak Weekend Market

ASIATIQUE THE RIVERFRONT
(0) *(🗺 0)*

South of the Taksin Bridge, an old warehouse on the river has been tastefully converted into a huge nighttime market. Alongside huge shops, you can check out the good restaurants, a ferris wheel *(admission 300 baht)* with a fantastic view and the popular travesty show at *Calypso Cabaret (shows daily 8:15 and 9:45pm | 900–1200 baht | tel. 0 26 88 14 15 | www.calypsocabaret.com). 2194 Charoen Krung Rd | free shuttle boat from Sathon Pier, Skytrain station Saphan Taksin | www.asiatiquethailand.com*

CHATUCHAK WEEKEND MARKET
★ (0) *(🗺 0)*

One of the largest markets in the world – not hard to believe once you've been round all 10,000 stalls – selling a truly mind-boggling array of goods. From guitars to garden implements, t-shirts to teapots, it's all here, and a paradise for those who just love to rummage around – almost half a million people every weekend. *Sat, Sun 6am–6pm | Paholyothin Rd | by the Mo Chit Skytrain station, Chatuchak Park metro station | www.chatuchak.org*

SIAM PARAGON ● (U D4) *(🗺 d4)*

Ultra chic shopping centre where you can get everything including a brand new Lamborghini. The selection is staggering – as are the ostentatious displays. There's also a giant aquarium, a luxury multiplex cinema and countless restaurants. *991 Rama I Rd | by the Siam Skytrain station | www.siamparagon.co.th*

INSIDER TIP SIAM SQUARE
(U D4) *(🗺 d4)*

A warren of alleyways with hundreds of shops: clothing, shoes, accessories at every turn. This is also the venue for young Thai designers to showcase their newest creations. The multilevel, air-conditioned *Siam Square One (www.siamsquareone.com)* is situated right in the middle and brings hundreds of shops under one roof. *Rama I Rd | across from the Siam Paragon Shopping Centre*

SPORTS & LEISURE

Learn the secrets of Thai cuisine in a cookery course, for example at the noble ● *Blue Elephant (from 3000 baht | 233 Sathorn Tai Rd | tel. 0 26 73 93 53 | www.blueelephant.com)* or at the *Baipai Thai Cookery School (2200 baht | course participants are picked up | tel. 0 25 61 14 04 | www.baipai.com).*

ENTERTAINMENT

INSIDER TIP ABOVE ELEVEN
(0) *(🗺 0)*

Stylish, modern and yet still cosy rooftop bar on the 33rd floor with a fantastic view of the city, delicious cocktails and snacks. The same applies for the related *Gramercy Park* a floor above. *Daily 6pm–2am | Sukhumvit Rd, Soi 11 | mobile tel. 08 35 42 11 11 | www.aboveeleven.com*

ROUTE 66 (0) *(🗺 0)*

Huge club with three floors (hip-hop, live Thai music and electro) and people ready to party. Bursting at the seams at the weekend. *Daily 8pm–2am | Royal City Av. | tel. 0 22 03 04 07 | www.route66club.com*

SIAM NIRAMIT (0) *(🗺 0)*

Thai art and culture is celebrated in a costume extravaganza with 150 actors in this huge show. *Daily 6–10pm, show begins at 8pm | admission 1,500 –2,000 baht, an additional 350 baht with buffet dinner | 19 Tiam Ruammit Rd | shuttle bus from the Thailand Cultural Center subway station| tel. 0 26 49 92 22 | www.siamniramit.com*

WHERE TO STAY

INSIDER TIP ARIYASOMVILLA
(U F4) (*f4*)
Centrally located but quiet accommodation with a lovely garden and pool plus individually furnished rooms. Very friendly service and a pleasant atmosphere. *25 rooms | 65 Sukhumvit Rd, Soi 1 | tel. 0 22 54 88 80 | www.ariyasom.com | Expensive*

ATLANTA HOTEL (U F4) (*f4*)
Legendary 1950s hotel with a "zero tolerance" policy towards sex tourists and drugs. Rooms are simple, spacious and clean. Nice garden with Thailand's oldest hotel pool. *59 rooms | 78 Sukhumvit Rd, Soi 2 | tel. 0 22 52 60 69 | www.theatlantahotelbangkok.com | Budget*

BAAN K RESIDENCE (U E5) (*e5*)
The spacious, apartment-like rooms offer every comfort and the staff is very helpful. It is worth paying the slightly higher price for the executive rooms. *28 rooms | 12/1 North Sathorn Rd, Soi 2 | tel. 0 26 33 99 11 | www.baankresidence.com | Moderate*

INSIDER TIP CASA NITHRA
(U B2) (*b2*)
Very pleasant and modern boutique hotel for backpackers with higher standards. Terrific view over the old town from the pool on the roof. *50 rooms | 176 Samsen Rd | tel. 0 26 28 62 28 | www.casanithra.com | Moderate*

SOFITEL SO BANGKOK (U E5) (*e5*)
Wonderfully designed luxury hotel with all the amenities and excellent culinary options. The rooms are impeccable beyond a doubt. *238 rooms | 2 North Sathorn Rd | tel. 0 26 24 00 00 | www.sofitel-so-bangkok.com | Expensive*

INFORMATION

BANGKOK TOURISM DIVISION (BTD)
(U A3) (*a3*)
BTD info booths can be found everywhere in the city. *Daily 9am–7pm | 17/1 Phra Athit Rd | near the National Theater | tel. 02 2 25 76 12 | www.bangkoktourist.com*

KANCHANABURI

(130 C5) (*C9*) **This provincial capital (pop. 50,000) 130 km (80 miles) west of Bangkok does not have much to offer on its own, yet it attracts foreign visitors in droves.**
The main reason is the world-famous Bridge over the River Kwai, the subject of the 1957 David Lean movie based on the novel by Pierre Boulle. The bridge was rebuilt after the war. The iron and concrete structure bears no resemblance to the wood and bamboo bridge featured in the movie, which, by the way, was not shot on the Kwai, but on Sri Lanka. Buses run to Kanchanaburi every 20 minutes from Bangkok's Southern Bus Terminal *(approx. 2.5 hours | 110 baht);* trains run daily at 7:50am and 1:55pm from Bangkok Noi Railway Station (in the city district Thonburi). Organised tours starting in Bangkok are offered by every travel agency for around 590–1190 baht.

SIGHTSEEING

BRIDGE OVER THE RIVER KWAI

The bridge is located 2.5 km (1.5 miles) west of the city centre. Public songthaew (pick-up trucks) will drop you there for 10 baht per person, and motorcycle taxis from 30 baht. Trains from Bangkok wait briefly at the bridge before continuing to the last station, Nam Tok.

WAR CEMETERIES

A total of 6,982 Allied prisoners of war are buried at the *Kanchanaburi War Cemetery* between the city and the bridge. On the banks of the Kwai, 2 km south of the city, is the *Chungkai War Cemetery* with an additional 1,750 graves. You can take a boat from the bridge along the river to get there; tours also take in the *Wat Tham Khao Poon* monastery and its stalactite caves.

THAILAND-BURMA RAILWAY CENTRE

This private museum recounts the history of the "Death Railway" with meticulous precision. Exhibits highlight the appalling conditions prisoners had to endure while clearing the railway route through the jungle. *Daily 9am–5pm | admission 120 baht | 73 Jaokannun Rd | www.tbrconline.com*

FOOD & DRINK

INSIDER TIP BLUE RICE RESTAURANT

This peaceful garden restaurant on the other side of the river serves excellent Thai cuisine. Enjoy the view of the boats floating past. *153/4 Moo 4 | Thamakham | tel. 034512017 | www.applesguesthouse.com | Budget–Moderate*

MANGOSTEEN CAFÉ AND BOOKS

Small and cosy café-restaurant with a diverse menu located on the tourist street that dishes up decent portions for a cheap price. A larger branch is located on the other side of the river near the Blue Rice restaurant. *13 Mae Nam Kwae Rd | mobile tel. 0817935814 | www.mangosteencafe.net | Budget*

Not suitable for Hollywood, but world famous: the Bridge over the River Kwai in Kanchanaburi

WHERE TO STAY

Book in advance for a weekend stay. Many of the resort hotels and raft accommodations have been set aside for package tours.

BAMBOO HOUSE

The moored house rafts 300 m below the bridge are idyllic, but spartan. More comfortable rooms in terraced houses and a bungalow. Beautiful garden. *19 rooms. | Soi Vietnam | tel. 034 62 44 70 | www.bamboohouse.host.sk* | Budget

FELIX RIVER KWAI RESORT

A somewhat faded luxury awaits you right on the river, only 100 m above the bridge. Two pools, sauna, fitness centre, tennis court. *254 rooms | tel. 0 34 55 10 00 | www.felixriverkwai.co.th* | Moderate–Expensive

INSIDER TIP ORIENTAL KWAI

A true gem awaits 17 km (10.5 miles) northwest of Kanchanaburi. Excellently-run and romantic little resort with immaculately clean and spacious bungalows, a pool and a very pleasant atmosphere. *12 rooms | 194/5 Moo 1 | Ladya | tel. 0 34 58 81 68 | www.orientalkwai.com* | Moderate–Expensive

LOW BUDGET

Bangkok bargain: dart through the city by Skytrain (BTS) and subway (MRTA) in air-conditioned comfort. A *Day Pass* allows you unrestricted travel – for 120–130 baht.

The historic park of *Old Sukhothai* covers almost 70 sq km (27 sq mi) – a long hike. Or, hire a bicycle, available in various guesthouses and at the park entrance (from 30 baht per day).

In Bangkok most travellers head straight for the guesthouses on the *Khao San Rd* **(U A–B3)** ***(🕮 a–b3)***. But even the more costly places on *Sukhumvit Rd* are still reasonable: The *Suk 11 Hostel* **(U F4)** ***(🕮 f4)*** *(Soi 11, Sukhumvit Rd | tel. 0 22 53 59 27 | www.suk11.com)* offers double rooms from 715 baht.

INFORMATION

TOURISM AUTHORITY OF THAILAND

Information for the entire province is available here. *14 Saeng Chuto Rd | tel. 0 34 51 12 00*

WHERE TO GO

INSIDER TIP ERAWAN WATERFALL

(130 B5) ***(🕮 B8)***

The waterfall, located 70 km (43 miles) to the northwest of Kanchanaburi in the 550 sq. km (135,900 acre) *Erawan National Park (daily 8am–4:30pm | admission 300 baht)* is one of the most beautiful in the country. Refreshingly cool water cascades over calc-sinter deposits on seven levels. There is a wonderful bathing area at the third level, but it is a sweaty 90 minute walk up to the last of the seven steps. Plan to visit in the morning when it is cooler and less full.

SANGKLABURI ★

(130 A4) ***(🕮 B7)***

Sangklaburi (pop. 15,000), the last town before the Myanmar border, is 230 km (143 miles) northwest of Kanchanaburi on the shores of the *Khao*

More beautiful than any pool designer could imagine: swimming fun at the Erawan Waterfall

Laem Reservoir with the spire of the temple of the flooded old Sangklaburi still visible above the water. Accomodation is in guesthouses like the *P. Guesthouse (34 rooms | Si Suwan Khiri Rd | tel. 0 34 59 50 61 | Budget)* or even with a pool at the *Samprasob Resort (43 rooms | 122 Nongloo | tel. 0 34 59 50 50 | www.samprasob.com | Budget–Expensive)*.

A must-see is the INSIDER TIP *Wat Wang Wiwekaram* temple complex, a unique fusion of Indian, Burmese and Thai architecture. The country's longest wooden bridge spans a 400 m wide arm of the lake over to the village *Waeng Khan*. On the Thai side of the famous Three Pagoda Pass 30 km/18.5 miles away at the border, set in the bleak mountain environment, is a line of three weather-beaten chedis. Rumour has it that foreign travellers should be permitted to cross the border to Myanmar in the near future – but you should always check your government's current travel advisories before planning to cross the border.

DEATH RAILWAY ★ ●

(130 B–C5) (*B–C 8–9*)

The construction of the railway from Kanchanaburi to Myanmar cost the lives of some 12,000 Allied prisoners as well as more than 80,000 Asian forced labourers. The most spectacular part begins after the Kwai bridge, as the train winds around cliffs, carried on a creaking viaduct high above the river near the village of *Wang Po*. The last stop, *Nam Tok (70 km/42 miles from the bridge | trains leave daily from Kanchanaburi at 6:07am, 10:35am and 4:26pm | 100 baht)*, is a sleepy town. If you would rather not go back by train, take a bus via the *Sai Yok National Park* to Sangklaburi.

SUKHOTHAI

(127 D6) (◫ C5) **Sukhothai, that means – besides the not very attractive new town – above all the first Thai capital, now a Historic Park with nearly 200 ruins, spread over an area of 70 sq km (27 sq miles).**

The park lies 13 km (8 miles) from the town of New Sukhothai (pop. 25,000), capital of the province of the same name, 427 km (265 miles) north of Bangkok. There are several buses a day to Sukhothai from Bangkok's Northern Bus Terminal; the nearest train station is at Phitsanulok, 50 km (31 miles) away. Bangkok Airways flies to the award-winning boutique airport Sukhothai several times a day from Bangkok.

The centre alone has some 35 well-preserved monuments spread over an area of 6 sq km (2.3 sq miles). However, the ruins do not have quite the impact as those of Ayutthaya, nor do they compare to the colossal Angkor Wat in Cambodia. When the Sukhothai kings took over stylistic elements of Khmer architecture, they shunned the idea of divine kingship practised by the rulers of old. Their buildings were more in keeping with the simplicity and lightness of Buddhist doctrine.

The Buddha statue in the ruins of Wat Mahathat in Old Sukhothai has aged gracefully

SIGHTSEEING

OLD SUKHOTHAI ★

The biggest and finest temple in Sukhothai is *Wat Mahathat*. Its principal features include the main chedi standing on a pedestal and numerous Buddha statues, some of which have been restored. Nearby are the three prangs of *Wat Si Sawai*, while just to the north of the formerly walled city centre, the chedi at *Wat Phra Phai Luang* stands on an island in an artificial pool. Next to that is *Wat Sri Chum*, famous for its enormous seated Buddha (11 m/36 ft high – the largest in Sukhothai) contained within the walls and wooden leaf doors of the mondop.

The temples at the park can be explored by bicycle, for example on an informative guided mountain bike tour with *Cycling Sukhothai (990 baht | mobile tel. 08 50 83 18 64 | www.cycling-sukhothai.com)*, who also offer tours around the countryside. *Daily 6:30am–6:30pm | admission 100 baht per zone (centre, north and west), ● Sun–Fri from 6pm admission free in the central zone*

RAMKHAMHAENG NATIONAL MUSEUM

The collection contains numerous Buddha figures and other exhibits from the Sukhothai period. *Daily 9am–4pm | admission 150 baht | at the park entrance*

FOOD & DRINK

Enjoy savoury meals at the *night market on the Ramkhamhaeng Rd* in New Sukhothai, for example at the popular INSIDER TIP *Rom Pho*. Simple food stalls directly at the park entrance serve local and Western dishes.

WHERE TO STAY

THE LEGENDHA SUKHOTHAI

This charming resort, located approx. 1.5 km/1 mile from the entrance to the Historic Park, uses a lot of wood and classic Thai design. Rooms have all modern conveniences, and there's a pool. *55 rooms | 214 Jarodvithi Rd | tel. 0 55 69 72 49 | www.legendhasukhothai.com | Moderate–Expensive*

LOTUS VILLAGE

Frenchman Michel, formerly a cultural attaché in Bangkok, and his wife Tan operate this popular resort of Thai-style teak houses on the edge of New Sukhothai. Simple and clean rooms are partially equipped with air conditioning and a refrigerator. Bicycle rental and tours available. *20 rooms | 170 Rajthanee Rd | tel. 0 55 62 14 84 | www.lotus-village.com | Budget*

INSIDER TIP RUEAN THAI HOTEL

The former guesthouse is now called a hotel, but it has remained a stylish small place to stay, with lovely, comfortable rooms in a two-storey building around a pool. *27 rooms | 181/20 Jarodvithi Thong Rd, Soi Pracharuammit | tel. 0 55 61 24 44 | www.rueanthaihotel.com | Budget–Moderate*

INFORMATION

TOURISM AUTHORITY OF THAILAND

130 Jarodvithi Thong Rd | opposite the Shell service station | New Sukhothai | tel. 0 55 61 62 28

WHERE TO GO

SI SATCHANALAI (127 D5) (*🕮 C5*)

56 km (35 miles) north of New Sukhothai is another historic park with temple ruins from the Sukhothai period. The area is not as extensive as at Sukhothai, but more pristine, and it is another Unesco World Heritage site. Si Satchanalai is not a popular tourist venue, yet it is its seclusion that makes the park attractive. A tour including a vehicle with a driver costs approx. 1,780 baht. On the way, in the village of *Sawankhalok,* you'll find the *SawanVoranayok National Museum (Wed–Sun 9am–4pm | admission 50 baht)* featuring Buddha statues and ceramics from the Sukhothai period.

THE NORTH

Beyond the beaches, the most popular travel destination in the kingdom is the North, even for the Thais. The cool air of the mountains, where peaks rise to 2,565 m (8,415 ft), provides welcome relief.
This is applicable only in the winter months, since during the warm season in March/April temperatures can reach 40°C/104 °F. Foreign tourists are especially fascinated by the ethnological diversity of the region.

CHIANG MAI

(126 C3) (*B3*) **The region's largest city, with a population of 170,000, is situated in the fertile valley of the Ping River. Founded in 1296, it was the capital city of the independent kingdom of Lanna, which existed until 1558.**
The tourist infrastructure as well as the air, train and bus connections to Bangkok, 700 km (435 miles) away, are excellent.

SIGHTSEEING

OLD TOWN ★
Behind the moat and the partially preserved brick city wall, the Old Town has managed to retain much of its charm. You will encounter a delightful temple every few minutes; admission is free everywhere. The once 86-m (282-ft) high chedi of *Wat Chedi Luang (Phrappoklao Rd)* was partially destroyed by an earthquake in 1545, yet it is still an imposing sight at half that height, a restored 42 m/140 ft.

 Photo: Wat Phra That Doi Kong Mu in Mae Hong Son

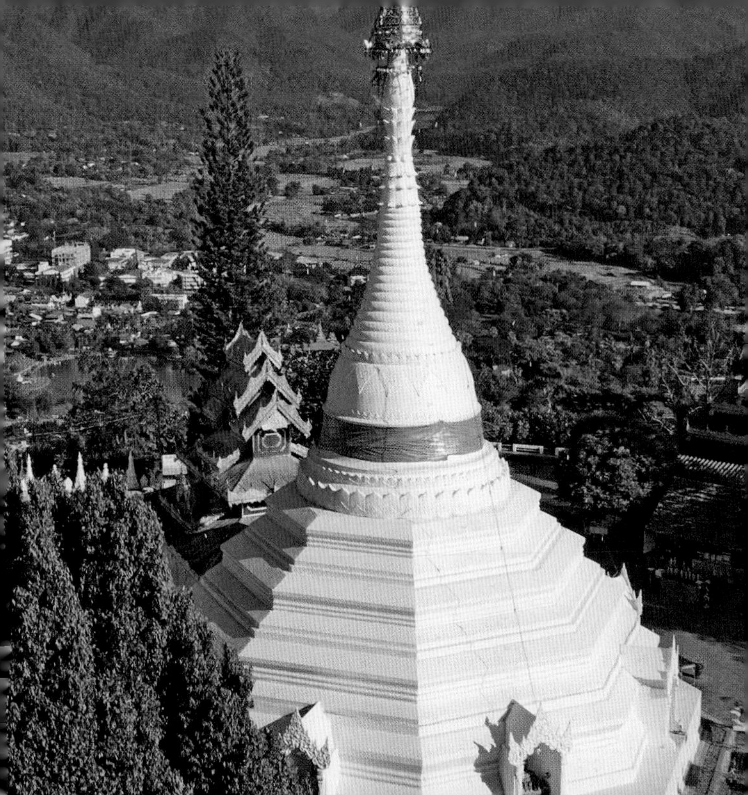

Adventure and culture: take a walk through the temple city of Chiang Mai and discover the land of the hill tribes

> CITY **WHERE TO START?**
> **Tapae Gate:** This gate takes you to the Ratchadamnoen Rd which leads straight to historic Chiang Mai. In the opposite direction Tapae Rd leads to the commercial centre of the town. Both areas can be easily explored on foot. If you're not staying in the town centre, let a Tuk-Tuk chauffeur you there.

Also well worth seeing is *Wat Chiang Man (Ratchapakinat Rd);* built in the same year the city was founded, it has exquisite carvings and wall paintings as well as elephant sculptures at the foot of the chedi. Another gem is *Wat Phra Sing (Sam Lan/Sigharat Rd)* with its unique library building, a masterpiece of timber construction.

MUSEUMS IN THE OLD TOWN

Three museums await visitors around the Sam Kasat Monument. The *Chiang Mai City Arts & Cultural Centre,* the *Chiang*

Explore the jungle on the back of an elephant in the area around Chiang Mai

Mai Historical Centre and the *Lanna Folklife Museum* provide background information on local history, culture and art. *Tue–Sun 8:30am–5pm | admission each 90 baht, joint ticket 180 baht | Phra Pokklao Rd | www.cmocity.com*

FOOD & DRINK

There are food stands at the *Galare Food Center* (featuring folklore dances in the evenings) across from the night market, as well as opposite the Chang Puak Gate in the north of the Old Town.

AROON RAI

If you are looking to try the classic northern Thai curry noodle soup INSIDER TIP *khao soi*, Aroon Rai is the place to go. This simple open restaurant has been serving inexpensive Thai cuisine for over 50 years. *45 Kotchasan Rd | tel. 053276947 | Budget*

LA FONTANA

Tasty pizzas and pasta are prepared in this authentic and inviting Italian restaurant at a good price. *Ratchamanka Rd 39/7–8 | tel. 053207091 | www.lafontanachiangmai.com | Budget–Moderate*

THE RIVERSIDE

Evenings feature really good live music at this terraced restaurant on the Ping River. As a novelty, order off the menu aboard the excursion boat *(75-minute river journey daily at 8pm). 9–11 Charoen-rat Rd | tel. 053243239 | www.theriversidechiangmai.com | Budget–Moderate*

SHOPPING

Handicrafts and needlework produced by the hill tribes are abundant, especially at the *night bazaar* on the *Chang Klan Rd* and at *Tapae Gate.* The street from the gate into the Old Town is closed to traffic on Sundays to make way for a vast market. The village of *Bor Sang*, east of Chiang Mai, is famous for its colourfully painted paper umbrellas and parasols. *Sankampaeng Rd,* leading there, is lined on both sides with shops offering an array of carvings, jewellery, silk, and souvenirs.

SPORTS & LEISURE

Different elephant camps around Chiang Mai offer guided tours. A recommendable option is INSIDER TIP *Elephant Special Tours (Mae Sopok | Aumpher Mae Wang | mobile tel. 08 61 93 03 77)*. They teach you how to steer these grey giants through the jungle and look them in the eye – a one-of-a-kind experience. A three-day package including room and board starts at 16,600 baht.

ENTERTAINMENT

There are small bar districts in the upper *Loi Kro Rd* near the Old Town and around the *Zoe in Yellow* in *Ratchawithi Rd.* Local students prefer the bars and clubs along the *Nimmanhaemin Rd* (close to the university), e.g. *Monkey Club* and *Warm Up.*

WHERE TO STAY

THE 3 SIS

Delightful lodge in the heart of the Old Town. All rooms are air-conditioned, equipped with refrigerators and TVs and done out in typical North Thai Lanna style. *24 rooms | 1 Phrapoklao Rd, Soi 8 | tel. 0 53 27 32 43 | www.the3sis.com | Budget–Moderate*

INSIDER TIP BAAN HANIBAH B & B

Stylish and tastefully decorated rooms are rented out in this old Lanna house made of teak. The quiet location in the Old Town as well as the lovely garden and the friendly personnel are a major bonus. *12 rooms | 6 Moon Muang Rd, Soi 8 | tel. 0 53 28 75 24 | www.baanhanibah.com | Budget–Moderate*

GALARE GUEST HOUSE

Pleasant rooms, fully equipped. Situated on the Ping River, and very good value for money. *33 rooms | Charoenprathet Rd, Soi 2 | tel. 0 53 81 88 87 | www.galare.com | Budget*

INSIDER TIP RACHAMANKHA

Reminiscent of a temple complex in the Lanna style, furnished with antiques – an

MARCO POLO HIGHLIGHTS

★ The Old Town of Chiang Mai
Masterpieces of temple construction behind ancient walls → p. 46

★ Doi Inthanon
Take a walk on top of Thailand's highest mountain → p. 50

★ Mae Hong Son
The ideal starting point for tours in the mountainous North → p. 53

★ Pai
The small city in the mountains attracts seasoned travellers with its alternative vibe → p. 54

★ Soppong
Heed the call of the adventurous caves near this village → p. 55

oasis of peace with a large pool near Wat Phra Sing. The rooms are tastefully simple, but elegantly furnished. *24 rooms | 6 Rachamankha Rd | tel. 053904111 | www.rachamankha.com | Expensive*

INFORMATION

CHIANG MAI MUNICIPAL TOURIST OFFICE
Tapae Rd | tel. 053276140

WHERE TO GO

DOI INTHANON ★
(126 B3–4) (*Ⓜ B4*)
A road leads right to the summit of Thailand's highest mountain (2,565 m/8,415 ft). In the national park of the same name it's possible to take excursions to

Wat Phra That Doi Suthep, one of the most famous monasteries in Thailand, is a good 700 years old

waterfalls and to see a hill tribe village. There is a chedi near the top; a nature trail leads through the fairy-tale cloud forest. There are some beautiful vistas as you drive up the mountain and it is interesting to observe the changing climatic zones within such a short space of time. Don't forget to take a jacket or pullover! *Admission 300 baht, tours from Chiang Mai from 1,400 baht | 100 km (60 miles) southwest of Chiang Mai*

LAMPHUN (126 C4) (*Ⓜ B4*)
Lamphun is a tranquil little place. Until 1281 it was the capital of the independent kingdom of Haripunchai. The main attraction is *Wat Phra That Haripunchai*, dominated by its enormous (51-m/167-ft high) gilded chedi. There is a small *National Museum (Wed–Sun 9am–4pm | admission 100 baht)* near the monastery. Lamphun has kept much of its old charm; largely untouched by tourism, it is a pleasant place

in which to relax and take in the atmosphere of a North Thai provincial town. *Bus service from Chang Puak bus station (500 m north of Chang Puak Gate) | 20 baht | 30 km (18.5 miles) south of Chiang Mai*

WAT PHRA THAT DOI SUTHEP
(126 C3) *(🕮 B3)*

This spectacular temple on Mt Suthep (1,676 m/5,499 ft) overlooking Chiang Mai is famous throughout Thailand. It is located at a height of 1,070 m (3,510 ft) and was built in 1338 as a repository for a Buddha relic. From the car park, a staircase with 306 steps flanked by mythical Naga serpent leads up there. If you're not up to that, there's always the funicular *(20 baht)*. Weekends attract hordes of Thai visitors. *Daily 8am–5pm | tour approx. 550 baht | public minibuses (50 baht) from Chang Puak Bus Station (500 m north of Chang Puak Gate) run daily until 3pm as a shuttle service | 16 km (10 miles) northwest of Chiang Mai*

CHIANG RAI

(127 D2) *(🕮 C2)* **Chiang Rai, capital of the province of the same name, was founded in 1262.**

The city of 67, 000 inhabitants is the economic hub of the far North, but it is much quieter than Chiang Mai.

SIGHTSEEING

HILLTRIBE MUSEUM

The Hilltribe Museum provides information on the culture of the six major tribal groups in Northern Thailand, and organises socially compatible trekking tours. *Daily 8am–6pm | admission 50 baht | Tanalai Rd | tel. 0 53 74 00 88 | www.pda.or.th/chiangrai/hilltribe_museum.htm*

INSIDER TIP WAT RONG KHUN

Buddha meets Batman in this surreal temple complex created by a famous Thai artist. Clad entirely in white, this masterpiece of architecture, sculptures and paintings is like no other temple in Thailand. *13 km/8 miles south on Hwy. 1 | admission free*

FOOD & DRINK

You'll find a large selection of food stalls at the *night market* in the city centre.

SHOPPING

The *night market* is not as large as the one in Chiang Mai, but the handicrafts and other products made by the hill tribe artisans cost rather less. Folklore dances are also staged here.

WHERE TO STAY

KANLAYA PLACE

Centrally-located, inexpensive and friendly accommodation with clean rooms. The rooms facing the street can be a bit loud due to the bars outside. *9 rooms | tel. 0 53 60 17 56 | 428/5 Jetyod Rd, Soi 8 | Budget*

THE LEGEND CHIANG RAI BOUTIQUE RIVER RESORT

Enjoy a dose of luxury in the northeast of the city thanks to your elegant and very spacious room plus the riverside infinity pool. *78 rooms | Moo 21 | 124/15 Kohloy Rd | tel. 0 53 60 79 99 | www.thelegend-chiangrai.com | Expensive*

INFORMATION

TOURISM AUTHORITY OF THAILAND

448/16 Singhaklai Rd | tel. 0 53 74 46 74

WHERE TO GO

MAE SAI (127 D1) (🕮 C2)

Thailand's northernmost city is located 65 km/40 miles from Chiang Rai on the Myanmar border. What was once a popular destination among backpackers is now one enormous market, with one tourist bus arriving after another. A bridge leads to *Tachilek (daily 6:30am–6pm | 500 baht for foreign day trippers)*. Modern rooms done in an unfinished concrete style await at the *After Glow Hostel (20 rooms | tel. 053734188 | www.afterglowhostel.com | Budget)* 4 km (2.5 miles) from the border.

INSIDER TIP MAE SALONG (127 D1) (🕮 C2)

This village (also called Santi Khiri, 67 km/41.5 miles northwest of Chiang Rai) on the 1,355-m/4,445-ft high Doi Mae Salong is inhabited by descendants of Chinese Kuomintang soldiers, who fled to Thailand through Burma (now Myanmar) after Mao Zedong's Revolution. They grow tea, coffee and vegetables. Teas and dried fruit from China are sold at the market which is also frequented by members of the various hill tribes. The *Chinese Martyr's Museum* is located at the entrance to the village. A comfortable place to stay with a fantastic view of the village is *Baan See See (24 rooms | tel. 053765053 | Budget)*.

SOP RUAK (127 D1) (🕮 C2)

The drug caravans that once monopolised the triangle between Thailand, Laos and Myanmar (the Golden Triangle) have now been replaced by buses full of tourists. The little village of Sop Ruak is packed with souvenir stalls. If you take a boat trip on the Mekong you can go ashore on the Laos side and pick up such exotic souvenirs as snake schnapps in the villages. *70 km (43 miles) north of Chiang Rai*

THATON (126 C1) (🕮 C2)

The village of Thaton located 70 km (43 miles) northwest of Chiang Rai is the starting and end point for rafting trips

The market in Mae Sai brings many tourists to Thailand's northernmost city

down the Kok river *(daily 10:30am from Chiang Rai, 12:30pm from Thaton, duration approx. 3 hours)*. It is also worth checking out the impressive *Wat Thaton* with its nine levels that overlooks the city. It is crowned by a 45 m high (150 ft) chedi, from which you can look across the entire area. Thaton itself has a few guesthouses, but the better quality resorts are found right on the river. They include the *Khun Mai Baan Suan Riverside Resort (29 rooms. | tel. 0 53 37 32 14 | www.khunmaibaansuan.com | Budget)*, which is gloriously situated on bend in the river.

MAE HONG SON

(126 B2) *(A3)* ★ **The smallest provincial capital in the country (pop. 20,000) is also one of the most idyllic.**

Near the Myanmar border and surrounded by mountains, Mae Hong Son's remoteness once earned it the sobriquet "The Siberia of Thailand". Be that as it may, the environs are perfect for those who like to go exploring off the beaten track.

SIGHTSEEING

On the picturesque *Chong Kam Lake* in the middle of the town are the filigree temples of *Wat Chong Klang* and *Wat Chong Kham (free admission to both)*. It is particularly romantic here when mist hangs over the lake in the early morning. There are breathtaking views from the monastery on the 424-m (1,391-ft) high *Doi Kong Mu*.

FOOD & DRINK

Food stalls are situated at the *night market* on the lake. Thai cuisine accompanied by live music can be found at the *Sunflower Café (Budget–Moderate)*; for good pizza try *Primavera (Budget–Moderatte)* in the south of the city centre on the main road.

FERN RESTAURANT

This large restaurant is Mae Hong Son's best, serving some exotic local dishes such as fried ferns. *87 Khunlumpraphat Rd | tel. 0 53 61 13 74 | Budget–Moderate*

WHERE TO STAY

INSIDER TIP FERN RESORT

This eco resort lies in a beautiful setting. It consists of comfortable, climatised wooden bungalows and there's a nice pool. The staff all come from the area, with some of them belonging to the Karen tribe. Only the freshest ingredients purchased at local markets are used in the kitchen. *36 rooms | Pha Bong | 9 km/5 miles outside the city | tel. 0 53 68 61 10 | www.fernresort.info | Moderate*

THE RESIDENCE @ MAE HONG SON

This three-storey wooden building to the northeast of the lake offers very clean rooms furnished with lovely teak furniture and other nice touches. *11 rooms | 41/4 Nivet Pisarn Rd | tel. 0 53 61 41 00 | Budget*

INFORMATION

TOURISM AUTHORITY OF THAILAND

4 Rajthampitak Rd | tel. 0 53 61 29 82

WHERE TO GO

Agencies (e.g. *www.rosegarden-tours.com)* and guesthouses offer interesting excursions and trekking tours as well as bamboo rafting on the Pai River. A typical day tour for two participants taking in hill tribe villages and a visit to the "long necks" costs between 980 and 1,500 baht per person.

VILLAGES OF THE "LONG NECK WOMEN" (126 A2) (*A 2–3*)

A dubious commercial tourist attraction are the people of the Padaung tribe, known as the *long necks.* They are a subgroup of the Karen who escaped from Myanmar and are now settled in three villages in Thailand. The term refers to the tribeswomen whose necks are stretched by means of brass rings. Even the Padaung speak in hushed tones about this "human zoo".

The people of Mae Aw cultivate tea in an idyllic setting - and serve it to their guests

INSIDER TIP MAE AW (130 B2) (*A2*)

The trip though wild and remote mountains to this photogenic Kuomintang village by a small reservoir is almost like a journey to the end of the earth. Opium was previously planted here, the inhabitants now live off tourism and their tea plantations. Savour freshly brewed tea and specialities of the Chinese Yunnan cuisine in the small restaurants. The village is officially called Ban Rak Thai, "the village that loves Thailand".

PAI

(126 B2) (*B3*) ★ **Pai (pop. 6,000) situated in a broad valley is fast gaining popularity as the stronghold of the traveller scene in the North.**

With its restaurants and souvenir stalls, tattoo studios, chill-out bars and a host of cheap places to stay, Pai is an ideal place for those looking for a fun time or just to hang out. Well worth a visit in the town are the Shan Temples of *Wat Luang* and *Wat Klang*. You can also go for a swim 8 km (5 miles) to the southeast at *Thapai Hot Springs (admission 300 baht)*.

FOOD & DRINK

There's good Thai food at *Na's Kitchen (Budget)* near the school and *Baan Benjarong (Budget–Moderate)* on the town's edge in the direction of Chiang Mai. Recommended: the organic cuisine at the *Good Life Restaurant (Budget)* as well as in *Om's Garden Café (Budget–Moderate)*.

SPORTS & LEISURE

Pai is the hub for trekking and white water rafting on the Pai River. A few dozen agencies offer their services.

ENTERTAINMENT

There are plenty of bars in Pai; many are fly-by-night, but there is always a party somewhere. The *Jiko Bar* right in the centre is equally popular with locals and tourists.

WHERE TO STAY

PAI VILLAGE BOUTIQUE RESORT & FARM

Well-maintained bungalows of wood and bamboo in a central location. Relax in the garden with its goldfish pond. *22 rooms | Sukhapibal 1 Rd | tel. 053698152 | www.paivillage.com | Budget*

INSIDER TIP REVERIE SIAM RESORT

If you want to splurge a bit, this is just the right place. Fantastic luxury rooms decorated in colonial style with antiques, two pools, very accommodating staff and an excellent restaurant. *18 rooms | 476 Moo 8 | Vieng Tai | tel. 053699870 | www.reveriesiam.com | Expensive*

RIM PAI COTTAGE

Rustic, comfortable wooden bungalows right on the river near the town centre. *20 rooms | tel. 053699133 | www.rimpaicottage.com | Budget–Expensive*

WHERE TO GO

SOPPONG ★ (126 B2) (*🗺 A–B 2–3*)

In the vicinity of the small, wild market town 43 km/27 miles west of Pai, there are several giant, largely unexplored caves. Take a few hours for an adventurous tour through the *Mae Lanna Cave (from 470 baht per person)* or cross the 500 m long (546 yd) stalactite cave *Tham Lot* 8 km (5 miles) north of Soppong on a bamboo raft *(665 baht for up to 3 people)*. Ask at the local hotels for more information about the tours. Nearby, Australian John Spiess has built rustic bungalows at the *Cave Lodge (tel. 053617203 | www.cavelodge.com | Budget)*. A comfortable place to stay in the village itself with a pool and the friendly hospitality of the owner Penh is *Little Eden Guesthouse (tel. 053617054 | www.littleeden-guesthouse.com | Budget–Moderate)*.

LOW BUDGET

For only 350 baht you can speed down the Kok River from Thaton to Chiang Rai – in a roofed motor boat *(daily around 10:30am, trip duration 3–4 hrs)*. But be warned: this trip is not very comfortable!

Nowhere in Thailand can you delve into the delights of Thai cuisine as cheaply as in Chiang Mai. The prices for a cooking class start at just 980 baht, for example, at the *Thai Farm Cooking School (Moon Muang Rd, Soi 9 | mobile tel. 0812885989 | www.thaifarmcooking.net)* situated on an organic farm.

By train to Chiang Mai: The journey is slow (approx. 12 hrs. for 751 km/466 miles), but there is no cheaper way of getting from Bangkok to the North. *From 121 baht (3rd class), sleeping berth from 593 baht | www.railway.co.th*

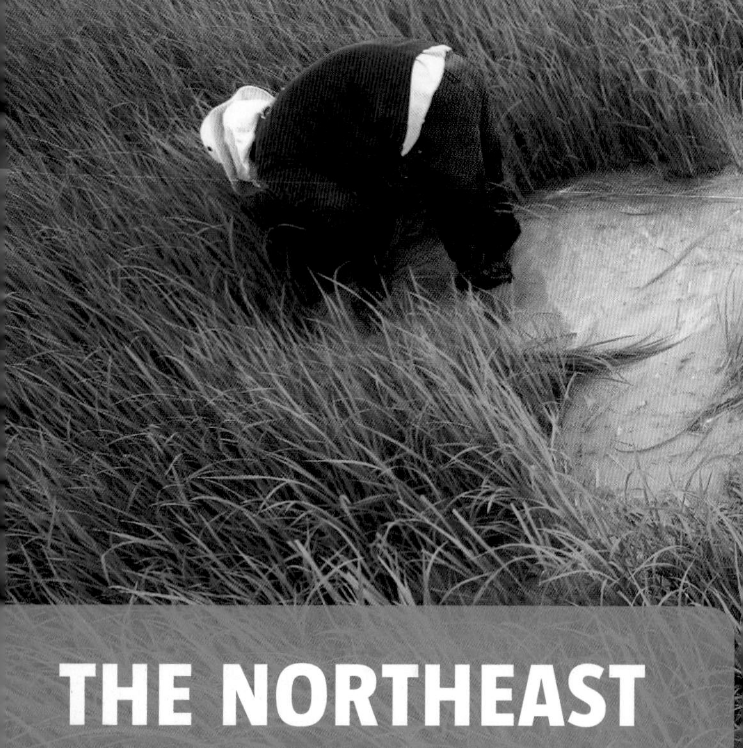

THE NORTHEAST

Similar to the Central Plains north of Bangkok, the High Plateau of the North-east is the land of the rice farmers.

But the region is prone to drought and has less fertile soil, the harvests are less reliable. Isan is known as the poorhouse of the nation, unable to feed all its people. For this reason many have migrated to the country's more prosperous areas.

KHON KAEN

(132 B2) *(🕮 F6)* **The city Khon Kaen (pop. 150,000) is located at the heart of Isan, about 450 km (280 miles) from Bangkok.**

Few tourists stop at this university city. Aside from the national museum and temples, the city itself has few noteworthy attractions.

SIGHTSEEING

BUNG KAEN NAKHON

This lake at the southeastern edge of the centre is a popular picnic area. By the lake is the enormous pyramid of INSIDER TIP *Wat Nong Waeng* with exquisitely carved details on doors and shutters.

NATIONAL MUSEUM

An extensive collection of archaeological artefacts including stone and bronze axes from Ban Chiang, a graceful bronze Buddha from the Sukhothai period, a Shiva statue from the 11th century, and even a

 Photo: Rice farmers

Where Thailand has retained its origins: in the land of rice farmers, on the trail of dinosaurs and ancient cultures

replica of a traditional farmhouse. *Wed–Sun 9am–4pm | admission 100 baht | Langsunratchakan Rd*

FOOD & DRINK

You can sample the wide range of typical Isan fare at the ● *night market.* Good Western food can be had at *Didine Restaurant (7/9 Pracha Samran Rd | Budget–Moderate)* round the corner of the Pullman Hotel.

ENTERTAINMENT

The central *Pracha Samran Road* has earned the nickname "Disco Street" thanks to its rather wild bar and dancing scene. One of the most popular places is the *Rad (231/2 Pracha Samran Rd)*.

WHERE TO STAY

KOSA HOTEL

The long-established city hotel is reasonably priced and has comfortable rooms. The facility is not the newest, but the rooms are in top form. *194 rooms | Srichan Rd | tel. 0 43 32 03 20 | www.kosahotel.com | Budget–Moderate*

WHERE TO GO

Tours can be difficult using public transport. Rent a vehicle instead (with or without a driver, from approx. 1,200 baht) at *Current Service (tel. 0 43 24 35 45)*.

A cobra is the star of the show in the village of Ban Khoksanga

INSIDER TIP PULLMAN KHON KAEN RAJA ORCHID

This is the best hotel in the city, offering five-star luxury in very comfortable rooms at bargain prices. The hotel has a pool and spa, five restaurants (Chinese, Italian, German, Thai, Vietnamese), a sushi bar and a karaoke bar. Kronen beer is brewed on the premises. *293 rooms | 9 Prachasumran Rd | tel. 0 43 32 21 55 | www.pullmankhonkaen.com | Moderate–Expensive*

INFORMATION

TOURISM AUTHORITY OF THAILAND

15/5 Prachasamoson Rd | tel. 0 43 24 44 98

PHU WIANG NATIONAL PARK ★

(132 A1) *(🕮 F6)*

This park has been dubbed "Dinosaurland". The life-size dinosaur models are recent, but the fossilised remains of the prehistoric beasts are 120–150 million years old. Follow the trails to the various digs, and study the fossil remains and information panels at the small Visitor Centre. *Admission 200 baht | 85 km (53 miles) northwest of Khon Kaen*

UBONRAT DAM AND COBRA VILLAGE

(132 B1) *(🕮 F6)*

The 800-m (0.5-mile) long *Ubonrat dam*, located 50 km (31 miles) northwest of Khon Kaen, has created a 410 sq km

(158 sq mile) reservoir – a favourite excursion destination with boat trips and a golf course. In the village of *Ban Khok Sa-nga* the *King Cobra Club* presents snakes in enclosures. Villagers step into the ring to pit themselves against the pythons and cobras. It's showtime as long as there are enough spectators; should you be the only visitor, negotiate a price in advance.

NAKHON RATCHASIMA

(132 A4) (*F7–8*) **Commonly known as Korat, the provincial capital is the largest city in the northeast with a population of 250,000.**

It is also the gateway to the province of Nakhon Ratchasima. The most interesting sights are to be found in the vicinity.

SIGHTSEEING

MAHA WIRAWONG NATIONAL MUSEUM

This museum's collection contains many Buddha figures, ceramics, carvings and examples of Khmer art. *Wed–Sun 9am–4pm | admission 20 baht | Ratchadamnoen Rd | at Wat Suthachinda*

THAO-SURANARI-MEMORIAL

Standing on top of her plinth, the bronze statue commemorates the brave wife of one of Korat's former governors. In 1826, Thao Suranari led the resistance against Laotian invaders and drove them out of the city. Also known as Khun Ying Mo, she is venerated as a saint by the people of Isan, and pilgrims come here every day to light incense sticks and place their offerings. *In the city centre between Ratchadamnoen Rd and Chumphon Rd*

FOOD & DRINK

You will find food stalls at the *night market (Mahattai Rd/corner of Manat Rd)*; good local cuisine is served in the stylish Thai beer garden at the *Ampawa Restaurant (264 Yommarat Rd | Budget–Moderate)* or, more cheaply, at *Happyland (280 Mahattai Rd | Budget) with noisy live music.* At *Chez Andy (closed Sun. | 5 Manat Rd | tel. 044289556 | www.chezandykorat.com | Budget–Moderate)* you can order a steak and hash browns.

WHERE TO STAY

DUSIT PRINCESS

The Princess is no longer in her prime, but is still the best hotel in the city. Spacious rooms with modern conveni-

MARCO POLO HIGHLIGHTS

★ **Phu Wiang National Park**
On the trail of dinosaurs at Thailand's own jurassic park → p. 58

★ **Khao Yai National Park**
A trek through the jungle with wild elephants → p. 60

★ **Phimai**
Thailand's most exquisite Khmer temples and ancient banyan trees → p. 60

★ **Elephant Round-up**
The festival in Surin showcases feats by jumbo elephants → p. 61

★ **Nong Khai**
A lovely town on the Mekong with a bridge to Laos → S. 61

ences and a large pool. *186 rooms | 1137 Suranarai Rd | tel. 0 44 25 66 29 | www.dusit.com | Moderate*

ROMYEN GARDEN PLACE
A large apartment block with fully equipped modern rooms outfitted with kitchenettes. *70 rooms | 168/9 Chomsurangyat Rd | tel. 0 44 26 01 16 | romyengardenplace.com | Budget–Moderate*

INFORMATION

TOURISM AUTHORITY OF THAILAND
Mittraphap Rd | on the bypass road at the edge of the city, near Hotel Sima Thani | tel. 0 44 21 36 66

WHERE TO GO

You can hire a car with driver, for example from *Korat Car Rental (136 Phonsaen Rd | tel. 0 44 39 37 30 | www.koratcarrental.com).*

SILK WEAVING VILLAGE
(132 A4) *(🕮 E8)*
The village of *Pak Thong Chai* is a major centre of Thai silk production, and you can watch how silk fabrics are woven by hand or produced with modern machinery. Dozens of companies ranging from small family businesses to high-tech manufacturers produce the precious material. If you buy your silk here you can be sure that it's absolutely pure. *32 km (20 miles) southwest | Shuttle bus service*

KHAO YAI NATIONAL PARK ★
(131 E–F5) *(🕮 E8)*
The oldest national park in the country – and one of the most beautiful – is also the largest elephant reserve. There are still around 200 elephants roaming in herds through the jungle here. You'll need a bit of luck to see them, though, and it's advisable to take a guide. There is a better chance that wild boars will cross your path or that hornbills will be flying overhead. From the *Park Headquarters (mobile tel. 08 60 92 65 29)* you can follow marked jungle trails without a guide, and stop at refreshing waterfalls on the way. You can also hire mountain bikes at the Park Headquarters. Organised tours to the park can be booked at many travel agencies. If you're on your own it's best to approach via *Pak Chong* (80 km/50 miles southwest of Korat) on Highway 2; from there it is a further 35 km (22 miles) to the park. There are a number of resorts along the access road and around the park, and these also offer tours. The *Samanea Resort (24 rooms, with pool | 100 Ban Lerd Thai | Moosee | Pak Chong | mobile tel. 08 37 23 77 74 | Moderate)* with its deluxe bungalows is beautifully situated on a hilltop. *Admission 400 baht pick-up service from Pak Chong*

PHIMAI ★ (132 B3) *(🕮 F7)*
This small town 58 km (36 miles) northeast of Korat is home to the largest Khmer temple complex outside Cambodia. At the *Phimai Historical Park (daily 7:30am–6pm | admission 100 baht)* imposing sandstone buildings surround the 92-ft-high central prang. Another worthwhile attraction is the *Phimai National Museum (Wed–Sun 9am–4pm | admission 100 baht)* filled with art and archaeological exhibits from the Isan region. And you can admire some of nature's wonders: the *banyan trees (Sai Ngam)* at the Mun River (1.5 km/1 mile to the east) are several hundred years old.
You'll find accommodation near the park at the modest *Boonsiri Guesthouse (13 rooms | Chomsudasadet Rd | tel. 0 44 47 11 59 | www.boonsiri.net | Budget)* with a pretty courtyard. They also organ-

ise tours, for example to the ruins of the Khmer temple in *Phanom Rung Historical Park*. Likewise centrally located but more comfortable and even with a pool is the *Pimai Paradise Hotel (42 rooms | 100 Samairuchi Rd | tel. 0 44 28 75 65 | www.phimaiparadisehotel.com | Budget)*.

SURIN (132 C4) (*G8*)

On the third weekend in November, this town of 40,000 inhabitants, capital of the province of the same name, is full of tourists here for the ★ *Elephant Round-Up,* when more than 300 elephants show off their skills. Travel agencies in Bangkok organise special excursions. In the village of *Ta Klang,* 60 km (37 miles) north of Surin is the non-commercial *Surin Elephant Study Center* that cares for 200 elephants and runs a museum about them. Volunteers are always welcome at the INSIDER TIP *Surin Project (www.surinproject.org)*.

Accommodation options in Surin include the slightly outdated *Petchkasem Grand Hotel (162 rooms | 104 Chitbamrung Rd | tel. 0 44 51 12 74 | www.pkhotel.co.nr | Budget)* with pool and restaurant. The sparsely furnished hostel *Pirom-Aree's House (9 rooms | 55 Thungpo Rd 326, Soi Arunee | tel. 0 44 51 51 40 | Budget)* is surrounded by a lovely garden; Pirom, a retired social worker, organises tours. Good, affordable local and Western food is served at the no-frills *Starbeam Restaurant (32/6 Soi Saboran 2 | Budget)*. *170 km (105 miles) east of Korat | arrival by bus or train*

Festivals for the large and not-so-large: Elephant Round-Up in Surin

NONG KHAI

(128 C4) (*F4*) ★ **This provincial capital (pop. 70,000), a stone's throw from Laos, promises a relaxing stay by the banks of the Mekong.**

A mythical world of rock at the sculpture park in Wat Khaek

The 1.7-km (1 miles) long *Thai-Laos Friendship Bridge* takes you to Vientiane, 26 km (16 miles) away. Trains run over the bridge, but the route to Vientiane is not completed yet.

SIGHTSEEING

INSIDER TIP SALA KAEW KU (WAT KHAEK)

This temple complex, with its bizarre sculpture garden, is quite unique. Visitors are dwarfed by an astonishing collection of giant Buddha statues, demons, Hindu gods and goddesses, seven-headed cobras, elephants and more. *3 km (2 miles) east*

FOOD & DRINK

In the *German Bakery (Koaw Woravut Alley | tel. 0 42 41 30 72)* you can get a hearty breakfast and delicious sweet rolls. The *Nagarina* floating restaurant *(www.nagarina.com | Budget)* casts off from below the Mut Mee Guesthouse everyday around 5pm (information at the guesthouse). The most romantic bar on the Mekong is also moored here: INSIDER TIP *Gaia (www.mutmee.com)* with regular live music. Food stalls open up in the evenings along *Prajak Rd* opposite the Wat Sri Saket.

SHOPPING

The very crowded *Indochina Market* on the river is chock-full of wares from Laos and China.

VILLAGE WEAVER HANDICRAFTS

There is a large selection of high-quality hand-woven fabrics and clothing at this self-help business project, at fair prices for the producers. *1151 Prachak Rd, Soi Chittanpanya*

WHERE TO STAY

INSIDER TIP MUT MEE GUESTHOUSE

Simple bungalows and rooms at this little oasis right on the river, with a good garden restaurant. You can also enrol in yoga classes or rent a bicycle here. *36 rooms | 111/4 Kaeworawut Rd | tel. 0 42 46 07 17 | www.mutmee.com | Budget*

ROYAL NAKHARA HOTEL

If you are looking for a dose of comfort, this hotel is the best in town. At Royal Nakhara Hotel, you can relax in spacious, clean rooms offering all the standard amenities at an unbeatable price. *80 rooms | 678 Saded Rd | tel. 0 42 42 28 89 | www.royalnakhara.com | Budget*

RUAN THAI GUEST HOUSE

This and other modest, family-run guesthouses can be found along Rimkong Rd (Lakeside road). *20 rooms | tel. 0 42 41 25 19 | www.ruanthaiguesthouse.nongkhaiinformation.com | Budget*

UDON THANI

(128 C5) (*F5*) **This major commercial centre (pop. 150,000) is situated on the railway between Khon Kaen and Nong Khai.**

Although the province is home to the country's most important archaeological site, near the village of Ban Chiang, the city itself is not a tourist destination.

WHERE TO STAY

KITLADA HOTEL

The rooms of the Thai-Chinese Kitlada Hotel are furnished in a functional and modern style. Unfortunately, the staff hardly speaks English. *40 rooms | Moo 7 | 510 Amphur Rd | tel. 0 42 24 55 42 | www.kitladahotel.com | Budget*

INFORMATION

TOURISM AUTHORITY OF THAILAND

16/5 Mukmontri Rd | tel. 0 42 32 54 06

WHERE TO GO

BAN CHIANG ★ (129 D4) (*G5*)

Around 3,500 years ago this small village 53 km (32 miles) east of Udon Thani was home to an advanced farming community. Excavations have unearthed grave goods including pottery and bronze implements alongside skeletons. An impressive INSIDER TIP *National Museum (daily 8:30am–4:30pm | admission 150 baht | www.penn.museum/banchiang)* has been created in collaboration with American experts. One excavation site can be seen in the courtyard of *Wat Po Sri Nai*. Hawkers sell pottery in front of the museum.

LOW BUDGET

Air conditioning, fridge, TV, DVD player, pool: In Nong Khai you'll find such accommodation from 600 baht at the centrally located *Pantawee Hotel (120 Rooms | 1049 Haisoke Rd | tel. 0 42 41 15 68 | www.thailand.pantawee.com).*

Bobby's Apartment & Jungle Tours (24 rooms | 291 Mittapab Rd | tel. 0 44 32 81 77 | www.bobbysjungletourkhaoyai.com) in Pak Chong takes you cheaply to the Khao-Yai National Park. Day trips with experienced guides cost 1,300 baht including admission. You stay in simple but spacious and very affordable rooms and are treated to good and generous meals.

EAST COAST

Between Bangkok and the Cambodian border, 400 km (250 miles) of coast await the visitors. Apart from the bustling international tourist playground of Pattaya, there are many smaller places at which to spend a relaxing beach holiday.

Heading east from Bangkok along Hwy 3, you'll pass through Thailand's largest industrial region, the Eastern Seaboard. But once you pass the salt ponds in Chonburi, the scenery starts to improve, and the holiday atmosphere returns completely on the stretch between Pattaya to Rayong. While tourists all over the world sun themselves on the beaches of Pattaya, at weekends and holidays those of Rayong are invaded almost exclusively by city-weary Thais. Beyond Rayong, for tourists a rather unappealing provincial capital, fishermen and fruit growers once more have the fertile coastal strip all to themselves. You will encounter only two more cities on the journey, Chantaburi, famous for its gemstones, and Trat, a springboard to Ko Chang. The second largest Thai island after Phuket (429 sq km/166 sq miles)) is the most beautiful place on the East Coast of the Gulf of Thailand for a beach holiday without the hype.

KO CHANG

(135 E–F4) (🕮 F11) ★ **Cloaked in jungle, peaks rising to 744 m (2,441 ft), a few fishing villages and palm-fringed beaches: this is the island of Ko Chang.**

 Photo: Lonely Beach at Ko Chang

Bustle or calm under the palms: the tourist capital Pattaya and the island of Ko Chang are vacation worlds apart

Even well into the 1990s Ko Chang was the haunt of backpack tourists who stayed in simple bamboo huts.

Since then, a tarmac road has been built along the beaches and through the jungle, and an undersea cable provides electricity from the nearby mainland. Resorts have sprung up like mushrooms. But you won't see any major construction in among the palm trees: on Ko Chang, you can still truly unwind.

Bangkok Airways flies from Bangkok to the provincial capital, Trat. An airport minibus will take you via ferry directly to the beach of your choice or the resort at Ko Chang. A minibus is the easiest means to travel from Pattaya (approx. 650–800 baht). Buses leave every hour from the Eastern Bus Terminal (Ekkamai) in Bangkok to Trat *(315 km/197 miles, trip duration 4–5 hrs)*. From there it is 30 minutes by *songthaeo* (public minibus) to the piers in the port town of Laem Ngob, where passenger ferries to Ko Chang and other islands operate all day. Most visitors now arrive on Ko Chang via the large piers in the bay of Thammachat, 15 km (9.3 miles) west of Laem Ngob.

SIGHTSEEING

Ko Chang is situated in a national marine park, where nature is still the biggest attraction. In the jungle, tired hikers can refresh themsleves at several waterfalls, the most beautiful of which is the three-tiered *Tan Mayom (admission 200 baht)* on the east coast near the park headquarters. It is most impressive during rainy season or shortly thereafter. The same goes for the *Klong Plu* waterfall *(admission 200 baht)* up behind Klong Phrao Beach. The fishing village of *Bang Bao* on the southern coast of the island was built on stilts in the sea. It is just the place for savouring fresh fish in an open-air restaurant. Take a boat tour and explore the 50 other islands that belong to Ko Chang's national park.

FOOD & DRINK

You will find the majority of independent restaurants on White Sand Beach. Dine on fine Italian cuisine at the friendly *La Dolce Vita (Moderate–Expensive)* but for the best breakfast on the island and everything from sausages in spicy sauce to green Thai curry, head to*Paul's Restaurant (Moderate–Expensive)*, located less than 500 m (500 yd) to the south. At night, the beach becomes a barbecue area as the resorts roll out mats for their guests and put up tables in the sand. A good, yet inexpensive option under the shade of the trees is *Sangtawan (Budget–Moderate)*.

Ko Chang has preserved much of its older, non-commercial charm

BEACHES

KAI BAE BEACH

The almost 2.5 km/1.5 mile long partially pebbled beach is said to be the most natural on the island. Behind it there is a pedestrian street with shops and pubs and a great lookout point on the southern end of the bay.

KLONG PHRAO BEACH

At almost 6 km (4 miles) this is the longest beach on the island. It's also the location of the largest resorts, all of them very peaceful since they're off the main road. But tourist infrastructure is rapidly being developed along the road.

LONELY BEACH (HAT THA NAM)

This beach is very pebbly with only a few hundred metres of sand, but with its zany chill-out bars and the cheapest accomodation on the island it is the place to go for backpack tourists helping to revive the hippie era. You'll need to hurry though: the first luxury resort has already opened.

WHITE SAND BEACH (HAT SAI KAO)

White Sand Beach in the north is the island's main beach: a narrow, 2.5 km/1.5 mile long strip of flatland between the jungle-covered mountains and the sea. Even at low tide it is not as flat as the beaches further south. The beach road is built up with resorts, bars, shops and travel agencies.

SPORTS & ACTIVITIES

Diving is increasingly popular, but even if you're only interested in snorkelling, you can still go along on a dive boat. Kayaks can be rented on the beach. Cruises to the surrounding islands and trekking tours through the jungle can be booked at any travel agency. In the village of INSIDER TIP *Salak Kok* on the east coast, the locals have started an initiative to preserve the Mangrove jungle. A nature trail *(free admission)* with English information boards takes you through this fascinating ecosystem. At high tide, you can also paddle through the mangroves in a kayak *(100–200 baht per hour)* Alternatively, sail across the crowns of the trees on ropes or hanging bridges at the *Tree Top Adventure Park (www.treetopadventurepark.com)* in the interior of the island.

ENTERTAINMENT

A few of the more unusual beach bars on White Sand Beach and Lonely Beach only close once the last guest has left. Long chains of fairy lights wound around bushes and palm trees create a festive atmosphere. Hip meeting places are the *Sabay Bar* (featuring full moon parties, live music and fire shows in the evenings) and *Oodie's Place* (live music). The restaurant terrace at INSIDER TIP *Rock Sand Resort*, set on a rocky outcrop at the northern end of White Sand Beach, is the best locale for enjoying a sundowner. Clusters of beer bars can be found right on the island road at White Sand Beach

MARCO POLO HIGHLIGHTS

★ **Ko Chang**
A lot of beaches, a lot of jungle and resorts for all budgets → p. 64

★ **Pattaya**
Numerous excursion destinations and activities: the city on the Gulf of Thailand has much more to offer than bars → p. 69

★ **Chantaburi**
Where precious gems are cut: day tours to the sapphire mines with a stopover at a mountain monastery → p. 73

Strips of sand between the jungle and the sea: White Sand Beach

and at Klong Phrao Beach *(Koh Chang Entertainment Complex)*. Lonely Beach has its own backpacker scene and is known as the party beach of Ko Chang. If you enjoy a lively nightlife, you've come to the right place.

WHERE TO STAY

Ko Chang is booming. Accommodation is scarce during peak season from December to February, so book well in advance. The prices here are still modest by Thai standards.

BANPU KO CHANG RESORT

A virtual South Sea paradise: palm-thatched, comfortable bungalows with TV, mini bar and a small pool – in the midst of a tropical garden on White Sand Beach. *31 rooms | mobile tel. 08 19 35 69 53 | www.banpuresort.com | Moderate–Expensive*

CENTARA KO CHANG TROPICANA RESORT

A very scenic facility in a tropical garden on Klong Phrao Beach. Spacious and stylish bungalows with every modern convenience, two pools. *157 rooms | tel. 0 39 55 71 22 | www.centarahotelsresorts.com | Expensive*

KLONG PRAO RESORT

Well-maintained bungalows (with TV and refrigerator) along a lagoon, only a few metres from the beach, plenty of space on the landscaped grounds. This resort is probably the most reasonably priced of all facilities on Ko Chang. *126 rooms | tel. 0 39 55 11 15 | www.klongpraoresort.com | Budget–Moderate*

PAJAMAS KOH CHANG HOSTEL

This stylish hostel on Klong Phrao Beach offers comfortable rooms as well as cheap beds with curtains in the air-conditioned dormitory plus a pretty pool. Very friendly staff. *22 rooms | tel. 0 39 51 07 89 | www.pajamaskohchang.com | Budget–Moderate*

INSIDER TIP **PORN'S BUNGALOWS**
A rustic resort right on Kai Bae Beach, shaded by old broad-leaved trees and coconut palms. A hot spot for travellers. Most of the modest bungalows are made of wood and have their own showers; there are also a few stone chalets with air conditioning. *26 rooms | mobile tel. 08 47 84 56 65 | www.pornsbungalows-kohchang.com | Budget–Moderate*

WHITE SAND BEACH RESORT
The oldest resort on Ko Chang is located on the peaceful northern end of the beach of the same name. Stilt bungalows with verandahs are simple but functional and are all equipped with air conditioning, TV and refrigerator. *92 rooms | mobile tel. 08 63 10 55 53 | www.whitesandbeachresort.net | Budget-Moderate*

INFORMATION

TOURISM AUTHORITY OF THAILAND
To the left in front of Laem Ngob Pier | tel. 0 39 59 72 55

WHERE TO GO

OASIS SEA WORLD *(135 E3) (🕮 F10)*
This is where you can swim with dolphins – but only if you have short fingernails and leave your glasses and jewellery behind (dolphins have sensitive skin!). The breeding station is located approx. 50 km (31 miles) west of Trat in Laem Sing. Dolphins that have been injured or tangled in nets are nursed back to health at the facility. Since there is a limited number of visitors permitted, booking in advance is highly recommended. *Admission 300 baht (including the show), 2,500 baht for swimming with the dolphins | several travel agencies also offer day tours | tel. 0 39 49 92 22 | www.swimwithdolphinsthailand.com*

PATTAYA

(134 C3) (🕮 D10) **Both famous and infamous, and written off by the media numerous times, ★ Pattaya is now more lively than ever. Nothing now remains of the sleepy fishing village that existed here in the 1960s.**

Pattaya is a seaside town, a mini metropolis of 260,000 inhabitants, noted for its vibrant nightlife. The countless bars which lend Pattaya the reputation as a hotbed of vice still exist. But the authorities are dedicated to improving this seedy image and have declared war on child prostitution. The once completely polluted bay of Pattaya has become much cleaner since a sewage plant was installed. However, it is now the kilometre-long Jomtien Beach that attracts swimmers, which is a 10-minute taxi ride away. There is also plenty of activity for the sports-minded: golf, diving,

CITY **WHERE TO START?**
Central Festival Shopping Centre: The shopping centre in the middle of Beach Rd is an ideal starting point for exploring the bay to the north and to the south. Baht buses (pick-ups with benches) drive down Beach Rd then back up along the parallel Second Rd (put your hand out to hail the bus, press the bell button to disembark; bus fare 10 baht, 20 baht at night). These two main roads have the most shops, restaurants, and hotels.

sailing, fishing, bowling, tennis, shooting, riding, go kart riding.

SIGHTSEEING

The list of tourist attractions in the province of Chonburi, where Pattaya is situated, is seemingly endless: offshore islands, sea aquarium, botanical gardens, folklore shows – one holiday is not nearly enough to see everything.

MINI SIAM

A large park showcasing the most famous buildings in Thailand and the rest of the world on a 1:25 scale. *Daily 7am–10pm | admission 250 baht, organised tour from a travel agency approx. 550 baht | on Sukhumvit Hwy., near the bus depot | tel. 0 38 72 73 33 | www.minisiam.com*

On the floating market in Pattaya

NONG NOOCH TROPICAL GARDEN

A zoo and folklore performances await you in the well-groomed botanical garden, which also boasts Thailand's largest collection of orchids. *Daily 8am–6pm, four shows between 9:45am and 4pm | admission 400 baht | 15 km/0 miles south of Pattaya | on the Sukhumvit Hwy. | www.nongnoochgardenpattaya.com*

PATTAYA FLOATING MARKET

The lake is artificial, likewise the stilt village in the middle of it. Although it was entirely designed for tourists, the Floating Market almost seems like a relic from the past. There are also more than 100 restaurants and shops, which are interconnected by bridges. *Daily 8am–8pm| admission 200 baht, boat tours 800 baht | in Southeast Pattaya, in the direction of Jomtien on the Sukhumvit Hwy. | www.pattayafloatingmarket.com*

RIPLEY'S BELIEVE IT OR NOT ●

Anything that is unbelievable, yet true, is on display here: from a three-legged horse to a mask made out of human skin to a Titanic constisting of 1 million matches. *Daily 11am–11pm | admission 590 baht | in the Royal Garden Plaza Shopping Centre (at the centre of Pattaya) | www.ripleysthailand.com*

SANCTUARY OF TRUTH

The world's tallest teak building lies in Naklua Bay and impresses with thousands of carved figures based on traditional Buddhist and Hindu motifs. The 100-m long and 100-m high monument explains Far Eastern mythologies and the relationship between man and the cosmos. *Daily 8am–6pm | admission 500 baht | www.sanctuaryoftruth.com*

FOOD & DRINK

BRUNO'S

An elegant restaurant with Swiss management serving excellent Mediterranean and Thai cuisine. *306/63 Chateau Dale Plaza | Thappraya Rd | Jomtien Beach | tel. 0 38 36 46 00 | www.brunos-pattaya.com* | Expensive

INSIDER TIP **MANTRA**

With everything from sushi and tandoori to bouillabaisse, the culinary delights of the East and the West come together here and are cooked before your eyes in the open kitchen. Tastefully decorated, plus a very appealing ambiance and excellent service to top it all off! *Beach Rd | nahe Soi 1 beim Amari Hotel | tel. 0 38 42 95 91 | www.mantra-pattaya.com* | Expensive

RUEN THAI RESTAURANT

Guests are entertained with classical Thai dancing at this open-air restaurant. *Pattaya 2 Rd | South Pattaya | tel. 038 42 59 11 | www.ruenthairestaurant.com* | Moderate

SHOPPING

Central Festival between Beach Rd and Second Rd offers the ultimate shopping experience: a gigantic emporium with 200 shops, restaurants, food stalls and cafés, an enormous supermarket, 16 bowling lanes and the luxury multiplex ● *SFX Cinema* with 10 screens. You will also find an array of shops and boutiques at the nearby *Royal Garden Plaza*. The *Mike Shopping Mall (262 Pattaya 2nd Rd)* is a large department store that resembles a covered bazaar.

Wood carvings at the Sanctuary of Truth

ENTERTAINMENT

Pattaya has a host of pubs with live music, including the *Green Bottle Pub (216 Pattaya 2nd Rd | at the Diana Inn Hotel)*, which is popular among the ex-pat community. *Club Insomnia (Walking Street)* and the modern *Mixx Discotheque (Bali Hai Plaza | south end of Walking Street)* are favourite clubs, but it is the rather gloomy *Marine Disco (Walking Street)* that is almost legendary. For sophisticated cocktails with a view of the city, take the lift to the 34th floor of the Hilton Pattaya, home of the *Horizon Bar (333/101 Beach Rd)*. For a completely different kind of experience with impressive costumes and spectacular stage sets, hit one of the travesty revues at

● *Tiffany's Show (admission 800–1200 baht | 464 Pattaya 2nd Rd | tel. 038 42 96 42 | www.tiffany-show.co.th)* and at the *Alcazar (admission 600–800 baht | 78/14 Pattaya 2nd Rd | tel. 0 38 42 22 20 | www.alcazarthailand.com).*

WHERE TO STAY

Out of all the Thai holiday destinations, Pattaya offers the best value for money: accommodation including TV, mini bar and pool in even the cheapest of accomodation is typical.

AUGUST SUITES

The August Suites features spacious, comfortably appointed rooms with balconies in a central location. Guests can also enjoy the delights of a pool, a sauna and a gym. It's a really good deal with prices starting at 40 euros. *79 rooms | Moo 9 | 111/43 Central Pattaya Rd | tel. 0 38 42 00 03 | www.augustsuites.com | Budget–Moderate*

HOTEL BARAQUDA

The design hotel is one of the hippest and most popular hotels in Pattaya. The spacious rooms have a contemporary and cool interior. The ☀ restaurant on the seventh floor enjoys a fantastic view. *72 rooms | Pattaya 2nd Rd | tel. 0 38 76 99 99 | www.hotelbaraquda.com | Expensive*

THAI GARDEN RESORT

Renowned child-friendly facility (playground, children's menu) with a large pool area and comfortable rooms as well as bread and cake from their own bakery. Five minutes by taxi to Wong Amat Beach. *227 rooms | 179 North Pattaya Rd | tel. 0 38 37 06 14 | www.thaigarden.com | Moderate–Expensive*

LE VIMAN RESORT

This small resort with well-maintained gardens and a pool offers clean, modern rooms with kitchenettes. Very friendly staff. *12 rooms | Moo 10 | Tappraya Rd,*

Pattaya buzzes with life at night under the neon lights of Walking Street

Soi 15 | mobile tel. 08 00 90 29 32 | le-viman-resort-pattaya.h-rez.com | Budget–Moderate

INFORMATION

TOURISM AUTHORITY OF THAILAND
Pratamnak Rd | direction Jomtien Beach | tel. 0 38 42 87 50

WHERE TO GO

CHANTABURI ★ (135 E3) (*F10*)
The provincial capital (pop. 140,000) 170 km (106 miles) southeast of Pattaya is famed for its sapphires and rubies. Most of the mines have been worked out and are now closed, but if you take a tour you can still see gem cutters at work. Although many stones today come from Cambodia, Chantaburi remains the centre of the Thai gemstone trade. A large gemstone market is located in the city centre. The French-style *Notre Dame* cathedral, the largest in the country, is also worth seeing. At the end of the 19th century, Vietnamese Christians emigrated to Chantaburi and introduced the colonial style which is still evident today in many houses. A stopover at the *Wat Kao Sukim* mountain monastery and the waterfall at *Khitchakut National Park* make an ideal day tour. *Tour from Pattaya incl. lunch approx. 2,000 baht*

KO LARN (134 C3) (*D10*)
Just 8 km (5 miles) from Pattaya, this island of 4 sq km (1.5 sq miles), with its white sandy beaches and clean water, is a popular local island excursion; there's quite a lot going on there. Travel agencies book island tours with excursion boats. Chartered speedboats will whisk you across for approx. 1500–3000 baht. The ferry from INSIDER TIP *Bali Hai Pier* in South Pattaya costs only 30 baht.

KO SAMET (135 D3) (*E10*)
The 20 sq km (8 sq mile) island is located 80 km (50 miles) southeast of Pattaya in the province of Rayong. Its scenic sandy beaches lure hordes of visitors from Bangkok on weekends. There are plenty of bungalow complexes, including the recommendable and appealing INSIDER TIP *Vongduean Resort (64 rooms | tel. 0 38 64 41 71 | www.vongdeuan.com | Moderate–Expensive)*, situated on the beach of the same name, that offers a free ferry service. The island is a national park, and foreigners have to pay a 200 baht entrance fee. *Minibuses take you to the fishing village Ban Phe for approx. 250–350 baht | Ferry trips 50–100 baht (30 minutes)*

LOW BUDGET

Air-conditioned buses depart for Pattaya every 30 minutes from the Ekkamai bus station in Bangkok (right by Ekkamai Skytrain station). A single journey costs 141 baht. A slower but less costly option (31 baht) is the train from the Bangkok main train station at 6.55am. Buses to Trat – and further on to Ko Chang – depart every hour for 248–272 baht (also from Ekkamai).

"Where you're not a stranger, just a friend we haven't met yet" is the motto of the *Elephant & Castle (6 rooms | 2 km (1.2 miles) south of White Sand Beach | mobile tel. 08 60 27 63 44 | www.elephantandcastlekohchang.com)* on Ko Chang. The Englishman John and his Thai team offer family-style hospitality and simple, clean bungalows with air-conditioning in a large tropical garden. Plenty of peace and quiet for 14–23 euros per night.

On the beaches and especially on the islands in the Guldf of Thailand and the Andaman Sea, holiday dreams come true for visitors from all over the world.

Nature has smiled upon the Thai people from the South. Even before the tourists arrived they enjoyed a life of relative ease: plenty of fish from the seas, fertile land as well as considerable mineral wealth (notably tin) endowed the region with prosperity and even affluence.

HUA HIN

(134 B3) (🗺 C10) **Kings went to stay in the country's oldest seaside resort when Thailand was still known as Siam. Today, the endless beaches are primarily the preserve of weekend visitors from Bangkok, 200 km (124 miles) away, and pensioners from Northern Europe.**

Since the end of the 1990s the town of 80,000 inhabitants has developed as a hotspot of international tourism, and it now features Western cuisine in the city centre. There are even a few bar streets, but many visitors are of an age where the charm of an old-fashioned seaside resort is more appealing than bar-hopping, although that charm starts to fade.

FOOD & DRINK

There are lots of restaurants serving international cuisine along *Naresdamri Rd* (parallel to the beach). There are also

Photo: Nang Thong Beach in Khao Lak

A vacation paradise above and below water: fantastic beaches, spectacular bays and some of the world's best diving

numerous fish restaurants, which present seafood to passers-by on a bed of ice. The best value food is to be found at the *night market* in the centre, where you can devour a delicious mussel omelette or noodle soup with duck, but also pricey lobster.

LA PAILOTE

Frenchman Christopher creates French and Thai delicacies, and also combines them. Tempt your palate with mussels with Roquefort cheese or crab curry. *174/1 Naresdamri Rd | opposite the main entrance of the Centara Resort | tel. 0 32 52 10 25 | www.paillote.net | Moderate–Expensive*

ENTERTAINMENT

Beer bars can be found along the *Soi Bintabat*, and there's live music in the *Hilton Resort Hua Hin (33 Naresdamri Rd)*. Classic Thai dances, mask and sword dances are showcased at *Sasi (Tue–Sun 7pm | 83 Nhongkae Rd | near the Hyatt Regency |*

Tourists from around the world now play where Siamese royals once splashed around in Hua Hin

mobile tel. 08 63 93 33 06 | www.sasirestaurant.com); a Thai dinner is included in the price of 750 baht.

WHERE TO STAY

There is a large selection of guesthouses and hotels situated between the beach and the city centre.

ANANTARA HUA HIN RESORT

An oasis with lovely tropical gardens and very luxurious, spacious and tastefully-decorated rooms plus a large pool. A variety of restaurants and several bars with live music also cater to guests. *187 rooms | 43/1 Phetkasem Rd | tel. 0 32 52 02 50 | huahin.anantara.com | Expensive*

CENTARA GRAND BEACH RESORT

Built in the 1920s, this colonial style hotel combines luxury with nostalgia against the backdrop of a beautiful park right on the beach. Rooms located in both the hotel wing and in detached villas. Several restaurants, among them the historic *Museum Coffee & Tea Corner,* four pools, spa and fitness centre. *249 rooms | 1 Damnernkasem Rd | tel. 0 32 52 02 50 | www.sofitel.com | Expensive*

HUA HIN AVENUE

A laid-back small hotel, good value for money. The rooms are comfortable and have an understated elegance. Guests can use the pool of the neighbouring hotel. Located in the city centre near the market. *11 rooms | 18/5 Sa Song Rd | tel.*

0 32 51 22 39 | www.huahin-avenue.com | Budget–Moderate

INFORMATION

TOURIST INFORMATION CENTER
Phetkasem Rd | on the turnoff to the street leading to the station | tel. 0 32 53 24 33

KHAO LAK

(136 C4) (*A15*) **The region 75 km (47 miles) north of the Phuket airport has long been a popular vacation spot for families and travellers seeking tranquility.**

Khao Lak was one of the coastal areas of Thailand hardest hit by the tsunami on 26 December, 2004. A small tsunami museum and a stranded police boat that was washed ashore (by the main road at Bang Niang Beach) commemorate the victims of the catastrophe. The resorts and infrastructure were subsequently reconstructed in record time. Khao Lak is the collective term for the 10-km (6-mile) stretch of beaches of *Khao Lak (Sunset Beach), Nang Thong, Bang Niang* and *Khuk Kak*. The main road (National Highway 4) runs parallel to the beach between 500–1,000 m back from the shore. Along the road are rows of restaurants and boutiques, dive shops, and everything else related to tourism.

FOOD & DRINK

Nick from Switzerland serves homemade bread for breakfast and cakes at *Bistro (main road to Bang Niang Beach | mobile tel. 08 62 77 09 19 | Budget–Moderate)*. For excellent INSIDER TIP thai curry and prawn soup, head to *Smile (Nang Thong Beach | mobile tel. 08 33 91 26 00 | www.smilekhaolak.com | Moderate)*. The *Khaolak Seafood Family House (Nang Thong Beach | tel. 0 76 48 53 18 | www.khaolak-seafood.com | Moderate)* rents out bungalows and dishes up delicious fish.

MARCO POLO HIGHLIGHTS

★ Ko Lanta
Despite the boom there is plenty of room on the beaches – the further south, the quieter → p. 79

★ Ko Jum
The only 9-km (6-mile) long jungle island of Ko Jum where your spirit is allowed to flow → p. 82

★ Ko Samui
The island of coconut palms in the Gulf of Thailand. Although Ko Samui has no cultural sightseeing attractions, it offers a variety of aquatic sports → p. 82

★ Phuket
Where travellers from all over the world meet: Thailand's diving centre and first class beaches as well as great views from the Big Buddha and the lighthouse on Cape Promthep → p. 88

★ Ko Phi Phi
Spectacular and absolutely idyllic: Phi Phi Don and Phi Phi Le are Thailand's most beautiful islands → p. 91

★ Phang Nga Bay
A stunning vista of rocky islands jutting out of the sea, plus caves and a stilt village → p. 91

SPORTS & ACTIVITIES

One of the world's best diving spots is only 50 km (31 miles) away: the *Similan Islands,* reached from *Tap-Lamu-Pier* south of Khao Lak. The excellent diving areas further north around the *Surin Islands* (60 km/37 miles from the mainland) are also quick to reach from Khao Lak. You can book tours to islands, caves and waterfalls in the jungle, such as the five-level and 200 m high (656 ft) INSIDER TIP *Chong Fah* in *Lamru National Park (admission 200 baht),* at travel agencies. Bang Niang Beach is also home to a *mini golf course (turn off the main road after the Tsunami Museum)*.

ENTERTAINMENT

Night life in Khao Lak is mostly limited to looking up at the starry sky. At the *Degree Bar (Bang Niang Beach)* and the *Happy Snapper (daily from 10pm | Nang Thong Beach),* there's live music. *O'Connor's Sportsbar (Nang Thong Beach)* has longer opening hours as well. Two travesty shows await along the main road at Bang Niang Beach: the *Moo Moo Cabaret (daily 9:45pm)* and the *Angel Ladyboy Cabaret (daily 9:30pm).* Although they are not quite as grand as the shows in Phuket or Pattaya, there is no cover charge.

WHERE TO STAY

Khao Lak is not ideal for budget travellers: you won't find a room on the beach for less than approx. 20 euros, and prices increase dramatically around the New Year period.

LA FLORA RESORT & SPA

A world-class resort with a range of luxurious rooms as perfectly styled as the whole complex. Beautiful pool and spa. *138 rooms | Bang Niang Beach | tel. 076428000 | www.laflororesort.com |* *Expensive*

GREEN BEACH RESORT

Simple, clean bungalows – all air-conditioned, with mini-bar and bamboo furniture – set in a scenic garden. The bungalows are placed rather close together, though this is the most reasonably priced resort for its beach location. *44 rooms | Nang Thong Beach | tel. 076485845 | www.khaolakbeach.com |* *Moderate*

KHAOLAK BHANDARI RESORT & SPA

Tastefully-furnished, spacious rooms full of amenities await you in beautiful Thai houses made of dark wood. The resort is set back from the beach, but surrounded by pretty gardens with a water lily pond and a pool. *77 rooms | Nang Thong Beach | tel. 076485751 | www.khaolakbhandari.com |* *Expensive*

NANGTHONG BAY RESORT

The family-friendly resort has well-maintained, comfortable rooms (with TV and fridge) in either a two-storey hotel wing or in bungalows. The resort has a pool as well as an exquisite garden. An unbeatable deal for Khao Lak. *80 rooms | Nang Thong Beach | tel. 076485088 | www.nangthong.com |* *Budget–Expensive*

INSIDER TIP POSEIDON BUNGALOWS

Ideal for those seeking peace and quiet. The modest bungalows (equipped with a shower, fan) are situated between the jungle and the beach. A small, eco-friendly hideaway, no trees were felled for the bungalows' construction, biodegradable waste is composted, and non-returnable bottles are frowned upon. The Swedish owners also organise diving tours to the Similan Islands. At km 53 (32 miles) from the direction of Phuket, a track branches off from the main road to the resort. *15 rooms | mobile tel. 08 78 95 92 04 | www.similantour.com | Budget*

WHERE TO GO

TAKUA PA OLD TOWN

(136 C4) (*⊞ B14*)

The small town of Takua Pa is a half-hour drive north of Khao Lak. It is divided into the bustling new town with a large market, and the sleepy *Old Town*. The latter provides a reminder of Takua Pa's glorious past, when, during the height of the tin boom in the early 20th century it even had a stint as the provincial capital. The many old buildings, built in Chinese and Sino-Portuguese style, testify to the town's former wealth, even if they have seen better days. It is said that the town's history goes back almost 2,000 years. It went by the name of Takola, and was said to be a major port from which merchant ships sailed to India and Arabia. To get to the Old Town along the river, follow national road 4032 from Takua Pa inland for 7 km (4.3 miles).

KO LANTA

(138 A3) (*⊞ B16*) **In the 1990s ★ Ko Lanta was the place to head for those who found Phuket too crowded and Krabi too limited.**

Time for a snack? The market of Ban Saldan on Ko Lanta has plenty of spicy options

But at the beginning of the new millenium, Ko Lanta experienced an enormous construction boom. Bamboo huts were replaced by a plethora of comfortable to luxurious bungalows. In the village of Ban Saladan, where the ferries dock, you'll find souvenir shops, tailors, cafés, travel agencies and dive shops. Ferries from Ko Phi Phi and Krabi will get you to Ko Lanta Yai in approx. one and a half hours; minibuses from Krabi take about two and a half hours including two ferry crossings, the first to the neighbouring island of Ko Lanta Noi which is not particularly interesting to tourists, and from there to Ko Lanta Yai.

LOW BUDGET

Bamboo huts on the beaches have become a rarity in the South. Great location directly on the beach:

Ko Samui: *Spa Samui Beach (tel. 0 77 23 08 55 | www.thesparesorts.net* at Lamai Beach has bungalows with showers and fans, some with air conditioning from 900 baht.

Phuket: *Ao Sane Bungalows (tel. 0 76 28 83 06)*, equipped with showers, is located in one of the most beautiful coves (Ao Sane). From 250 baht.

Ko Lanta: *Where Else (tel. 0 75 66 70 24 | www.lanta-where-else.com)* could easily pass for a set from a hippie movie. Huts with showers and fans from 500 baht.

Ko Jum: *Bo Deng Bungalows (tel. 08 14 94 87 60)* at Andaman Beach has huts with and without showers from 150 baht.

FOOD & DRINK

Ban Saladan has several seafood restaurants occupying old houses built on stilts over the water. Bakery/café *Nang Sabai* on the main road 1 km outside the town offers German bread and delicious cakes. *Same Same But Different (Budget–Moderate)*, at Kantiang Bay, serves international cuisine.

BEACHES

All bathing beaches are situated on the 20-km (13-mile) long west coast Ko Lanta Yai. As a rule of thumb, the further south you travel the quieter it gets. The last two beaches in the bays of *Klong Jak* and INSIDER TIP *Mai Pai (Bamboo Bay)*, which are reached along a partly steep road, are virtually untouched by tourism; there are only a few bungalows, and the jungle extends all the way to the beach.

SPORTS & ACTIVITIES

The resorts and travel agencies provide jungle and mangrove tours as well as snorkelling excursions and caving. Ban Saladan has numerous dive shops (an overview of the best diving spots can be found at: *www.lantainfo.com*).
When you book mangrove tours in the village of *Tung Yee Peng (tours from the travel agency 1,000 baht)* on the north east coast, you'll also be supporting a programme sponsored by the United Nations. The villagers want to integrate tourism into their daily lives without destroying their natural environment of mangrove forests and coastal waters. Boat tours operated by the locals will give you the chance to get to know the ecosystem from which the islanders have lived for many genera-

Peace and quiet in the South: hanging around on Ko Lanta

tions. In Tung Yee Peng you can enjoy simple accommodation and immerse yourself in village life.

ENTERTAINMENT

Trendy meeting places at Long Beach include the *Ozone Bar* and *Funky Monkey*. Or catch the fire shows at several beach bars in the evenings. Information on current events at *www.fb.com/groups/lanta*.

WHERE TO STAY

BAMBOO BAY RESORT

Modest hillside bungalows. A fine clifftop restaurant with views over the secluded bay. *21 rooms | tel. 0 75 66 50 23 | www.bamboobay.net | Budget–Moderate*

COSTA LANTA

Minimalist upscale bungalows constructed of concrete and old wood are surrounded by high casuarina trees. You'll either be repulsed or delighted by their architecture. Expansive premises and a large pool. *22 rooms | Klong Dao Beach | tel. 0 75 68 46 30 | www.costalanta.com | Expensive*

INSIDER TIP LAYANA

This elegant resort provides guestrooms in luxurious pavillions. Equipped with a spa, a saltwater pool with a view of the sea, a huge open-air jacuzzi and fitness area against a backdrop of a wide beach front and plenty of greenery. *50 rooms | Long Beach | tel. 0 75 60 71 00 | www.layanaresort.com | Expensive*

NICE'N EASY HOUSE

This nice mini resort is situated in a slightly hidden place, but directly on the beach. You can stay in air-conditioned wooden bungalows or in rooms at the terraced house. A small pool provides refreshment during the daytime. *10 rooms | Klong Khong Beach | tel. 0 75 66 71 05 | www.niceandeasylanta.com | Moderate*

RELAX BAY RESORT

Traditionally designed bungalows with stylish interiors overlooking a small, separate bay located at the south end of Long Beach. All rooms have air conditioning and fans; French and Thai cuisine. Overpriced during peak season. *45 rooms | Long Beach | tel. 0 75 68 41 94 | www.relaxbay.com | Moderate–Expensive*

Paradise in Thailand's South: Lamai Beach on Ko Samui

WHERE TO GO

KO JUM ★ ●
(138 A2) (*M B16*)

This 9-km (5.6-miles) long island (20 km/13 miles north of Ko Lanta) is in the shadow of the main tourism developments, but has still benefited from the Lanta boom. There are a couple of dozen small resorts here. Known in its northern part as Ko Pu, it is an island of jungle and rubber plantations; there is one paved road leading from north to south, the power poles were only erected in 2010. Today, the main village of *Ban Ko Jum* in the far south will supply you with all your daily needs. For your journey to Ko Jum, take the ferry from Krabi to Lanta, where longtail boats pick up travellers. *New Bungalow (27 rooms | Andaman Beach | tel. 08 97 26 26 52 | www.kohjumonline.com/new.html | Budget)* offers modest bungalows. Some are quite spacious, not all are equipped with showers. Englishman Ray and his wife, Sao, operate the pleasant *Woodland Lodge (14 rooms, equipped with showers | Andaman Beach | mobile tel. 08 18 93 53 30 | www.woodland-kohjum.tk | Budget)* noted for its outstanding cuisine. Located on a scenic hillside you'll find the INSIDER TIP *Oonlee Bungalows (9 rooms | Kidong Beach | mobile tel. 08 72 00 80 53 | www.kohjumoonleebungalows.com | Budget–Expensive)*. Valerie (Lee), originally from France, and her husband, Oon, ensure a pleasant ambience to accompany their appetising meals. The *Freedom Bar* and the *Coco Bar* at the southern end of Andaman Beach are both beach bars with a campfire.

KO SAMUI

(137 E3) (*M C14*) ★ **Ko Samui is Thailand's third-largest island (population: 50,000). As you approach by air, the impression is of one massive coconut plantation crowned by a jungle-covered mountain. Even the little airport has a rustic feel, at first glance looking more like a beach resort.**

There is lush green everywhere, with white sandy beaches and coves stretching round the coast like pearls on a string.

SIGHTSEEING

The 247 sq km (95 sq mile) island can be explored in a day via its 51-km (32-mile) long ring road. On the way you will pass two of the island's famous rocks: *Hin Ta* and *Hin Yai* at the southern end of Lamai beach. The "Grandmother rock" and the "Grandfather rock" have the shape of male and female genitalia. Local legend has it that an elderly couple were drowned when shipwrecked off the coast in a storm, turning into rocks to be remembered here forever.

In the south of the island it is well worth taking a detour up into the mountains to the INSIDER TIP *Secret Buddha Garden (admission: 80 baht)* near the Tar Nim waterfall. This is a magical world of weathered Buddha statues set in a rocky jungle landscape. Equally worthwhile is a trip to the island's landmark, the 12-m (39-ft) high *Big Buddha,* as well as the *Hin Lat* and *Namuang waterfalls.* The fishing village *Hua Thanon* in the southeast of Ko Samui features colourfully painted boats with intricately carved prows.

FOOD & DRINK

Thai cuisine from food stalls such as those at the *Lamai Food Center* or in neighbourhood restaurants is often better (and less expensively) prepared than in restaurants that cater to tourists. At Chaweng Beach, several resorts set up tables and chairs on the beach in the evening and grill seafood on charcoal fires. Foodies and romantics will feel like they are in paradise at the beautifully-situated restaurant *Tree Tops (Chaweng Beach | tel. 0 77 96 03 33 | lawana-chaweng.anantara.com/tree-tops | Expensive)* belonging to the Anantara Resort. Excellent, authentic Italian meals are served at INSIDER TIP *Duomo (Chaweng Beach | tel. 0 77 41 42 58 | Expensive).*

BEACHES

The most resorts and the best infrastructure can be found on *Chaweng Beach,*

On another level: Big Buddha, the landmark of Ko Samui

the most beautiful, and on *Lamai Beach* on the east coast of the island The bays of *Thong Sai, Choeng Mon, Chaweng Noi, Coral Cove* and *Na Khai* are small oases of tranquility. *Mae Nam, Bo Phut* and *Big Buddha* beaches on the north coast are likewise free of overwhelming tourist hype. The southern and western regions of Ko Samui are still poorly developed. Beaches in these areas are not especially attractive, and the shallow water is not really suitable for swimming.

SPORTS & ACTIVITIES

You have the choice of various aquatic sports on Ko Samui, the largest selection of which is found at Chaweng Beach and Lamai Beach (links to diving companies can be found at *www.kohsamui.org*). There are mini-golf courses at Chaweng Beach and on the road from Choeng Mon to the Big Buddha Beach. If you're in the mood for a proper game of golf, the island has four full-length courses to choose from *(www.samui.sawadee.com/golf)*.

ENTERTAINMENT

Chaweng Beach is the centre of the island's nightlife. At the *Green Mango(www.thegreenmangoclub.com)*, clubbers dance. Beer and go-go bars are a few doors down. The atmosphere is more relaxed and rustic at *The Rock Bar (www.samuirockbar.com)* on the beach. Travesty shows are put on at *Starz Cabaret (Chaweng Beach)* and *The Cabaret (Lamai Beach)*.

WHERE TO STAY

EDEN BUNGALOWS

Intimate resort with French management, set in a lush tropical garden with pool. The fully equipped rooms are either in bungalows or in the main Thai House. Two minutes away from the beach. *15 rooms | Bo Phut Beach | tel. 077427645 | www.edenbungalows.com | Moderate*

HARRY'S BUNGALOWS

Located at the northern end of Mae Nam Beach near the pier where the ferry departs for Ko Phangan, you will find plenty of greenery and tranquility around these very clean and cosy bungalows with air conditioning. *22 rooms | tel. 077247431 | www.harrys-samui.com | Moderate*

LAMAI PERFECT RESORT

The resort is an excellent value for money. Guests stay in well-kept, spacious rooms with all the amenities. Splash around in the pool or walk two minutes to the beach. *30 rooms | Lamai Beach | tel. 077424406 | www.lamaiperfectresort.com | Budget–Moderate*

THE LIBRARY

A cool design hotel: luxury rooms in white cubes, a red tiled pool, and plenty of green. Enjoy breakfast on the beach on white mats. *26 rooms | Chaweng Beach | tel. 077422767 | www.thelibrary.co.th | Expensive*

THE WATERFRONT

Friendly, small-scale hotel located directly on the beach with a tidy garden,

a pool and comfortable rooms perfect for relaxing the day away. *18 rooms | Bo Phut Beach | tel. 077427165 | www.thewaterfrontbophut.com | Moderate–Expensive*

INFORMATION

TOURISM AUTHORITY OF THAILAND
Nathon | Chonvithee Rd | behind the post office | tel. 077420504

WHERE TO GO

ANG THONG NATIONAL PARK
(137 E3) *(◫ C13–14)*
The archipelago of 40 uninhabited islands between Ko Samui and the mainland is ideal for snorkelling. Travel agencies offer day tours; one of the most interesting ones to consider is an exploration of the marine park by kayak.

KO PHANGAN (137 E3) *(◫ C13–14)*
Ko Samui's smaller neighbour (191 sq km/74 sq miles), reachable by ferry in 30 minutes, is a mountainous jungle in the sea surrounded by fine sandy beaches and small coves. What was once considered the destination for backpackers and hippies has been usurped by the mainstream tourist industry. More and more air-conditioned bungalows are replacing old palm leaf huts, while upscale resorts with pool and spa await more affluent travellers. A prime location is the *Santhiya (99 rooms | Thong Nai Pan Noi Beach | tel. 077428999 | www.santhiya.com | Expensive)*. Reasonably priced accommodation is available at all beaches, for instance, the lovely *Phangan Rainbow Bungalows (25 rooms | tel. 077238236 | www.rainbowbungalows.com | Budget)* are on Ban Kai Beach. Ko Phangan's monthly *Full Moon Party (www.fullmoon.phangan.info)* is now world famous, attracting thousands of revellers to *Rin Beach (Hat Rin)*.

KO TAO (137 E2) *(◫ C13)*
The crystal clear waters around this former penal colony is said to provide the best diving in the entire Gulf of Thailand. The 21 sq km (8 sq mile) island boasts more than 30 dive shops. There is probably no where else on the planet where as many people learn to dive as here.
Ko Tao is a green mountain ridge rising out of the the sea and tends to attract young travellers. There are a few upscale resorts here – such as the *Woodlawn Villas*

Delve into the midst of 40 isolated islands on a kayak tour in Ang Thong National Park

(8 rooms | near Sai Ri Beach in a park | mobile tel. 08 44 45 96 72 | www.woodlawnvillas.com | Moderate–Expensive) – and more modest accommodation on the main beaches of *Mae Hat* and *Sai Ri* as well as in small bays, e.g. the laid-back *Sairee Cottage (45 rooms | Sai Ri Beach | tel. 0 77 45 61 26 | www.saireecottagediving.com | Budget–Moderate)* with diving school on the premises. Ferries cross from the mainland (Chumphon) and from Ko Samui (via Ko Phangan).

KRABI

(138 A1–2) *(🕮 B15–16)* **This mainland province east of Phuket has the most stunning coastal scenery in all Thailand.** Particularly spectacular are the limestone cliffs flanking the prime beaches of Phra Nang and Railay, which are only accessible by boat *(from the main beach Ao Nang in approx. 20 minutes)*. The beaches get busy during high season. It is much quieter on the beaches of Klong Muang, Noppharat Thara and Tup Kaek, as well as in Ton Sai Bay.

SIGHTSEEING

KRABI TOWN

The cosy provincial capital (pop. 26 500) is situated at the estuary of the Krabi River. There is a selection of modest guesthouses as well as a few hotels, but so far the place hasn't been overrun by tourists. On the riverbank right in the centre you can charter a longtail boat to explore the mangrove forests on the opposite bank. From Uttarakit Rd, the main road across from the Grand Mansion Hotel, turn off along the INSIDER TIP ● *Mangrove Forest Walkway*. The boardwalk leads you approx. 400 m through a mangrove forest on the town side of the Krabi River.

PHRA NANG CAVE AND PRINCESS LAGOON

In the ● *Phra Nang Cave (free admission)* on Phra Nang Beach stands a shrine surrounded by huge wooden

Krabi's coast shines with white sand, lush green jungles and the turquoise blue water of the ocean

phalluses (lingams), a fertility symbol. People leave offerings here in order to be blessed with children or other good fortune. After an arduous ascent to the top of the 150-m (500-ft) high cliffs, you can see the lagoon below, which at high tide is filled with seawater.

INSIDER TIP WAT TAM SUA

Located 6 km (4 miles) outside Krabi Town, Wat Tam Sua (Tiger Cave Temple) is a meditation monastery, partly integrated into the caves of the temple mountain. The biggest attraction is the climb up 1,273 very steep steps to the top, from where there are breathtaking views.

FOOD & DRINK

For good yet cheap food head to the nighttime market in Krabi Town. Seafood restaurants line the beachside lane known as *Soi Sunset*, right at the narrow north end of Ao Nang Beach. The *Last Café* on the southern end of the beach has an idyllic location. Ao Nang Beach can be reached by bus from Krabi Town.

SPORTS & ACTIVITIES

Watersports enthusiasts have plenty of opportunities for diving and kayaking in the area (list of diving centres at: *www.aonang.com)*. Climbers can test their stamina on the towering limestone formations. Courses for beginners are offered at Phra Nang Beach, Railay East and at the Ton Sai Bay *(information: www.railay.com/railay/climbing/climbing_intro.shtml*).

ENTERTAINMENT

Krabi beaches are not known for their nightlife. Travellers tend to meet at pubs in Railay East and in the *Freedom Bar* in Ton Sai's hinterland. That's where beach parties take place, with full moon celebrations going on all night.

WHERE TO STAY

INSIDER TIP AO NANG HOME STAY

Mr Chang runs a very hospitable and family-style accommodation on Ao Nang Beach. The rooms are quite small, but immaculately clean, comfortable and well-kept. Located about ten minutes from the beach on foot. *6 rooms | Ao Nang Rd, Soi 11 | mobile tel. 0817321273 | www.aonanghomestay.com | Budget–Moderate*

DEE ANDAMAN HOTEL

Modern hotel in Krabi Town with spacious rooms and a pool. The Dee Andaman is one of the best hotels in the city and offers a good value for money. *30 rooms | 45/19 Rattanadilok Rd | tel. 075622998 | www.deeandamanhotel.com | Moderate*

NAKAMANDA

This beautiful resort features upscale villas surrounded by lush greenery and old trees. For the ultimate in luxury take one of the gigantic villas with its own private pool. Spa and swimming pool for all guests. *39 rooms | Klong Muang Beach | tel. 075628200 | www.nakamanda.com | Expensive*

RAILEI BEACH CLUB

A real refuge from the crowds of tourists who come to Railay beach for the day. The beautifully furnished private houses situated within a large park on the white sand beach are rented out to holidaymakers. *30 rooms | Railay West Beach | mobile tel. 0866859359 | www.raileibeachclub.com | Expensive*

SOMKIET BURI RESORT
Comfortable two-storey villas in a magnificent tropical garden with pool and a lovely cliff backdrop. Approx. 10 minutes from the beach. *26 rooms | Ao Nang Beach | tel. 075637990 | www.somkietburi.com | Moderate–Expensive*

INFORMATION

TOURISM AUTHORITY OF THAILAND
Krabi Town | Uttarakit Rd | tel. 075622163

PHUKET

(136 C5–6) (*B15–16*) **On ★ Phuket, Thailand's largest island (543 sq km/210 sq miles), dozens of first class beaches await you.**

In addition to its beautiful beaches, Phuket has a diverse landscape, a vibrant provincial capital and a host of recreational activities. It's no wonder Phuket (population: 320,000) has become Southeast Asia's number one holiday island.

SIGHTSEEING

BIG BUDDHA
The 45-m (148-ft) high Buddha sitting atop the *Nagarked* hill above Phuket Town is Thailand's tallest Buddha and the island's newest landmark. Its construction is being funded exclusively by donations. The site won't be finished for years to come, but a visit is a must. From the top you have a fantastic view over Phuket's east coast. *Free admission | shortly after Chalong on the road to the airport (signposted)*

KAO PHRA THAEO NATURE RESERVE
Located in the north of Phuket, this park contains the only remaining virgin rainforest on the island. A hiking trail leads to waterfalls. At the *Gibbon Rehabilitation Center (www.gibbonproject.org)*, gibbons abused as housepets are prepared for a return to their natural habitat.

CAPE PROMTHEP
Tourists by the busload clamour to photograph the sunset from the southernmost point of the island. Avoid the melee and go up to *Promthep Cape Restaurant (tel. 076288084 | Moderate)* and enjoy the view. The *lighthouse (free admission)* at the cape offers the best panorama.

PHUKET AQUARIUM
You are surrounded by sharks, giant sea perch and countless small fish (in a glass tunnel)! Experience the sublime flora and fauna from the waters of Phuket up close. *Admission 100 baht | near Phuket Town/Kap Phan Wa | www.phuketaquarium.org*

PHUKET TOWN
Many buildings in Sino-Portuguese style still stand in the attractive town centre (pop. 60,000); they recall the era of the rubber and tin barons. The carefully restored shop fronts on *Krabi Road* at the corner of Satun Road and the large Taoist temple *Bang Niaw (Phuket Road)* speak to the affluence of the residents back in the day.

FOOD & DRINK

INSIDER TIP CHINA INN CAFE
Thai cuisine and cappuccino taste especially good in this beautifully restored town house with a courtyard. *Phuket Town | 20 Thalang Rd | tel. 076356239 | Budget–Moderate*

KA JOK SEE
Outstanding Thai cuisine in an atmospheric old town house. Later in the evening, the restaurant turns into an inviting bar play-

Gibbons tumble about the treetops in Kao Phra Thaeo Park

ing tasteful music. *Phuket Town | 26 Takua Pa Rd | tel. 0 76 21 79 03 | Moderate*

MOM TRI'S KITCHEN

High above the sea between Kata and Kata Noi, a delicious combination of Thai and Mediterranean fare is served. *12 Kata Noi Rd | tel. 0 76 33 35 69 | www.villaroyalephuket.com | Expensive*

SHOPPING

The largest shopping centre on the island is the *Jungceylon (www.jungceylon.com)* at Patong Beach, complete with a department store and many smaller shops and restaurants. Another large plaza, the *Central Festival (www.centralfestivalphuket.com)* lies on the road from Phuket Town to Patong.

BEACHES

The most developed beach on Phuket is *Patong Beach.* With all its big hotels, however, it is also really crowded. *Karon* and *Kata* beaches are slightly less busy, while the beaches of *Ao Sane, Bang Tao, Kamala, Karon Noi, Kata Noi, Nai Harn, Nai Yang, Naithon, Pansea* and *Surin* are relatively quiet.

SPORTS & ACTIVITIES

All kinds of watersports are available on Phuket. The island is the centre of Thailand's diving tourism, since the water quality in the Andaman Sea is generally better than that of the Gulf of Thailand (links for diving spots can be found at *www.phuket.com/diving*). You can also swing and climb through the treetops on ziplines at *Flying Hanuman (Kathu | tel. 0 76 32 32 64 | www.flyinghanuman.com)* or go for a bungee jump with *Jungle Bungy Jump (Kathu | tel. 0 76 32 13 51 | www.phuketbungy.com)* Other options include mini-golf (Patong, Kata), golf (several courses), shooting and riding (Chalong).

ENTERTAINMENT

With its countless bars, Patong Beach is the stronghold of the island's nightlife. Opulent transvestite shows are the main event at *Phuket Simon Cabaret (700–800 baht | www.phuket-simoncabaret.com)*. A classy disco is *Seduction (www.seductiondisco.com)*. The gigantic theme park *FantaSea (admission from 1,800 baht | www.phuket-fantasea.com)* on Kamala Beach is a top attraction with its magical costume extravaganza. The folklore show with its museum village in *Siam Niramit Phuket (admission from 1,500 baht | Chalermprakiet Rd (Bypass Rd) | www.siamniramit.com)* is also quite huge. You can listen to good live music at the very popular *Timber Rock (118 Yaowaraj Rd)* in Phuket Town.

WHERE TO STAY

There are only a few resorts located directly on the beach. Booking in advance is advised, especially during the New Year season as well as the Thai and Chinese New Year celebrations.

INSIDER TIP BAIPHO

This boutique hotel is a gem. Each of the comfortable rooms styled by Swiss fashion photographer Rudi Horber is a work of art. *19 rooms | Patong | 205/2–13 Rat Utit 200 Pee Rd | by Hotel Montana Grand | tel. 0 76 29 20 74 | www.baipho.com | Budget–Expensive*

FANTASY HILL BUNGALOWS

These peaceful, friendly and shady bungalows lie on the hill between the Kata and Karon beaches. It is only a ten minute's walk from Fantasy Hill to both of them. The spacious rooms and bungalows are furnished in Thai style. *34 rooms | 8/1 Karon Rd | tel. 0 76 33 01 06 | sites.google.com/site/fantasyhillbungalow | Budget–Moderate*

ROYAL PHUKET CITY

Begin exploring the island from the best hotel in the city. It is definitely a better value for money than the places at the beach. It features a pool, gym, sauna and spa plus a café with a cake shop. *251 rooms | Phuket Town | Phang Nga Rd | close to the centre | tel. 0 76 23 33 33 | www.royalphuketcity.com | Moderate*

BOOKS & FILMS

The King and I – King Mongkut was unfairly portrayed as bad tempered and naive in this fictionalised account of his court. The film is still banned in Thailand, along with the 1946 film "Anna and the King of Siam" and the more recent film "Anna and the King" starring Jodie Foster.

Nana Plaza – Christopher Moore took the title of his mystery novel from a bar district in Bangkok. Full of suspense and local colour.

The Beach – Director Danny Boyle filmed this drama with Leonardo Di Caprio on the island of Phi Phi Le. An exciting storyline with stunning landscape cinematography.

Ong-Bak – He is Thailand's absolute superstar: Tony Jaa, actor and kickboxer. In these cult flicks directed by Prachya Pin-kaew, he fights his way through Bangkok on the search for a stolen Buddha head.

Best snorkelling conditions in the crystal clear water off Ko Phi Phi

TWINPALMS PHUKET

Elegant architecture and luxurious rooms, some of which have their own private pool, from which you can swim into the big pool. Here you can relax at the trendy INSIDER TIP *Catch Beach Club (www.catchbeachclub.com). 97 rooms | Surin Beach | tel. 076316500 | www.twinpalms-phuket.com |* Expensive

INFORMATION

TOURISM AUTHORITY OF THAILAND

Phuket Town | 191 Thalang Rd | tel. 076211036

WHERE TO GO

KO PHI PHI ★

(136 C6) (*B16*)

A jungle mountain in the azure blue sea, towering limestone cliffs and glorious white beaches greet you to Phi Phi. The 2004 tsunami destroyed the island village, but it has since been rebuilt; bungalows, pubs, shops and dive shops are in demand as never before, which is fatal for the environment. In season, Phi Phi also attracts daytrippers from Phuket und Krabi. They flock to the village on main island of *Phi Phi Don* to snorkel in the crystal clear water and take in the splendour of untouched *Phi Phi Le*, where Leonardo Di Caprio trudged through its powdered sand in the film "The Beach". There are plenty of rooms, but it's all abit crowded in the village and not the best value for money. For a more economic alternative, try *Papaya Phi Phi Resort (36 rooms | tel. 075818730 | www.papayaphiphi.com |* Moderate*)* for a comfortable stay.

PHANG NGA BAY ★

(136 C5) (*B15*)

Bizarrely-shaped limestone islands and islets jut out of the sea to heights of up to 300 m (1,000 ft). The best-known island is *James Bond Island* which featured in the movie "The Man with the Golden Gun". Stalactite caves and the stilt village of *Ko Panyi* are additional worthwhile attractions. Tours of the bay can be booked at any travel agency.

DISCOVERY TOURS

1 THAILAND AT A GLANCE

START: ➊ Phuket Town END: ⓭ Mae Sai	19 days Driving time (without stops) 50 hours
Distance: ➡ 2,840 km/1,765 miles	

COSTS: approx. 2,700 euros for 2 people (accommodation, food & drink, rental car, petrol and guided excursions)
WHAT TO PACK: navigation system or smartphone with GPS, swim gear, sun protection and mosquito repellent/nets

Experience the many different facets of Thailand on this cleverly devised route from south to north. Leaving touristy Phuket behind, you'll visit breathtaking natural highlights, amazing beaches and a royal residence before coming to the

 Photo: Ayutthaya

Every corner of the earth has its own special charm. If you want to explore all the many different facets of this region, head off the beaten track or get tips for the best stops, breathtaking views, hand-picked restaurants or the best local activities, then these customised discovery tours are just the right thing. Choose the best route for the day and follow in the footsteps of the MARCO POLO authors – well-prepared to navigate your way to all the many highlights that await you along the tour.

metropolis of Bangkok with the royal palace and the best shopping in all of Southeast Asia. Travel through former royal cities further to the north of the country where charming temples and spectacular mountain ranges will cast you under their spell.

DAY 1–2

1 Phuket

Your tour begins with two days on 1 **Phuket** → p. 88. Thailand's most beloved holiday island not only has an international airport serviced by all the major car rental agencies, but also a dozen amazing beaches worth writing home about. After exploring the fascinating old cen-

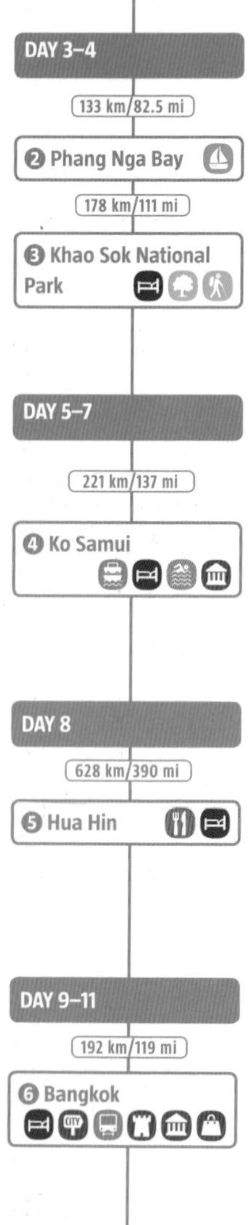

tre of **Phuket Town** with its Chinese temples and old Sino-Portuguese style villas, **drive south to the impressive Big Buddha**. Afterwards, spend a relaxing day at the **beach of Patong** before attending a transvestite show at the **Phuket Simon Cabaret**. Spend both nights at the artsy boutique hotel **Baipho**.

On the third day, take National Road 402 and Route 4 to Phang Nga on the mainland. At ❷ **Phang Nga Bay** → p. 91, embark on a boat excursion to the imposing rock islands that even left an impression on James Bond. Once you've docked, **follow highways 4, 415 and 401 into the jungle of ❸ Khao Sok National Park** → p. 100. Check into the beautifully-situated **Khaosok Rainforest Resort** *(28 rooms | tel. 0 77 39 51 35 | www.krabidir.com/khaosokrainforest | Budget–Moderate)*, where you will spend a total of two nights. The next morning, take off on a hiking tour through the jungle for the day.

Day 5 begins with a **drive along National Road 401 to Don Sak harbour to catch the car ferry over to ❹ Ko Samui** → p. 82. Enjoy all the comforts of **The Waterfront** for three nights. This little hotel sits directly on Bo Phut Beach. **The ring road around the island will take you to all the beaches.** Make sure to light a few incense sticks at the **Big Buddha** and admire the colourful fishing boats in the village of **Hua Thanon**. First and foremost, take time to unwind and clear the cobwebs from your head.

On the eighth day of the tour, **take the first ferry back to the mainland and drive the long stretch north along Route 4 to the royal seaside resort of ❺ Hua Hin** → p. 74. The seafood restaurants right on the water more than make up for the rather strenuous drive with fish fresh from the grill. All the charm of the 1920s awaits you in the luxurious **Centara Grand Beach Resort**, one of the oldest hotels in the country.

The tour continues along Route 4 and National Road 35 on the ninth day, bringing you to Thailand's vibrant capital, ❻ **Bangkok** → p. 35. Leave your rental car at your stylish accommodation **Ariyasomvilla** and explore the metropolis for three days **using public transport.** The fabulous **Grand Palace** and the **Wat Pho** are absolute must-sees for anyone visiting the capital. You can shop till you drop in the area around the Skytrain station Siam. If you happen to be in Bangkok at the weekend, you should definitely plan to walk over the gigantic **Chatuchak Weekend Market**.

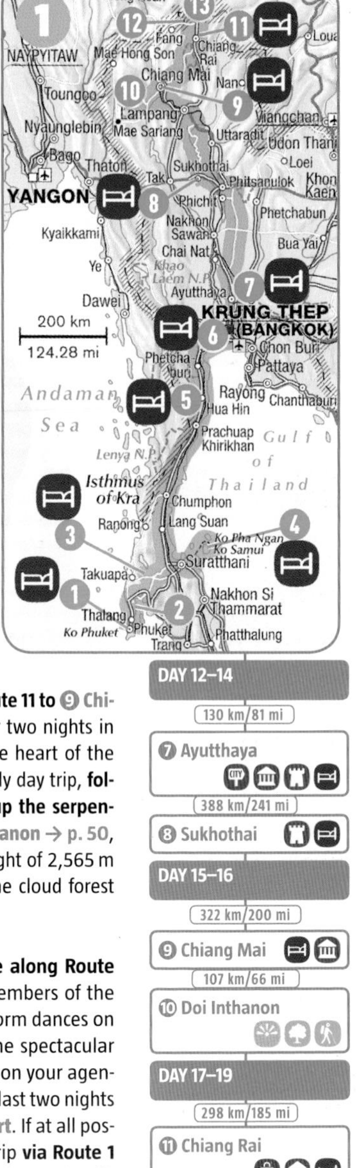

Leave Bangkok on Route 1 heading north to your first stop on day 12, the old royal city of ⑦ **Ayutthaya** → p. 33, which is only about one and a half hours away. This historic city is dotted with the ruins of temples and palaces – it is particularly enchanting at night when it is lit up by spotlights. After spending the night in the large **Kantary Hotel**, head out the next day **further north, following Route 32 first and then Routes 11 and 12 over the broad Menam plain, the rice basket of the country, to** ⑧ **Sukhothai** → p. 44. In the capital of the first Thai empire, **Old Sukhothai**, around 200 ruins in the historic park attest to the former glory of the "dawn of happiness" as this temple city was called when it was founded in 1238. The charming **Ruean Thai Hotel** will be your home for two nights.

On day 15, **take National Road 101 and Route 11 to** ⑨ **Chiang Mai** → p. 46, where you will stay for two nights in the attractive **Baan Hanibah B & B** in the heart of the quite impressive old city centre. For a lovely day trip, **follow Route 108 to the west, then drive up the serpentine National Road 1009 up to** ⑩ **Doi Inthanon** → p. 50, the highest mountain in Thailand at a height of 2,565 m (8,415 ft). Go for a small hike through the cloud forest near the summit.

Depart Chiang Mai on day 17 and drive along Route 118 further to ⑪ **Chiang Rai** → p. 51. Members of the mountain tribes sell handicrafts and perform dances on the **night market** in the city. A visit to the spectacular "white temple" **Wat Rong Khun** must be on your agenda if you're visiting Chiang Rai. Spend the last two nights of your tour in luxury at **The Legend Resort**. If at all possible, you should definitely take a little trip **via Route 1 and National Road 1089 into the mountains to the vil-**

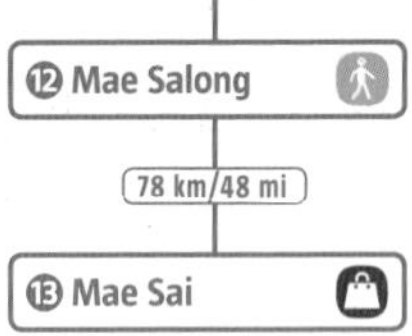

lage of ⑫ Mae Salong → p. 52. Descendants of Chinese Kuomintag soldiers now cultivate coffee and tea here. Walk through the village and enjoy its truly unique atmosphere. **At the end of Route 1,** you will come to Thailand's northernmost city, **⑬ Mae Sai → p. 52**, which is separated from Myanmar by the narrow river of Tachilek and just an hour's drive from Chiang Rai. Countless shops and market stalls line both banks of the river. After returning to Chiang Rai, you can catch a plane at the airport back to Bangkok or to another destination in Thailand.

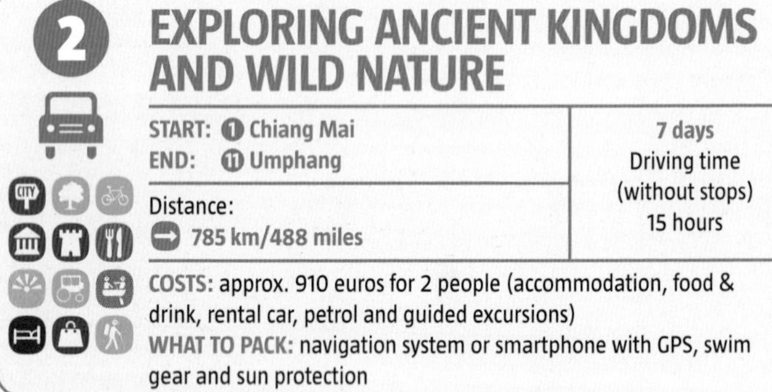

2 EXPLORING ANCIENT KINGDOMS AND WILD NATURE

START: ① Chiang Mai
END: ⑪ Umphang

Distance:
785 km/488 miles

7 days
Driving time (without stops)
15 hours

COSTS: approx. 910 euros for 2 people (accommodation, food & drink, rental car, petrol and guided excursions)
WHAT TO PACK: navigation system or smartphone with GPS, swim gear and sun protection

Follow the traces of ancient kingdoms and explore the rugged mountains on the border to Myanmar on this route leading south from Chiang Mai. You'll encounter sweet-tempered elephants, ride in a horse-drawn carriage and keep fit with mountain bike and rafting adventures.

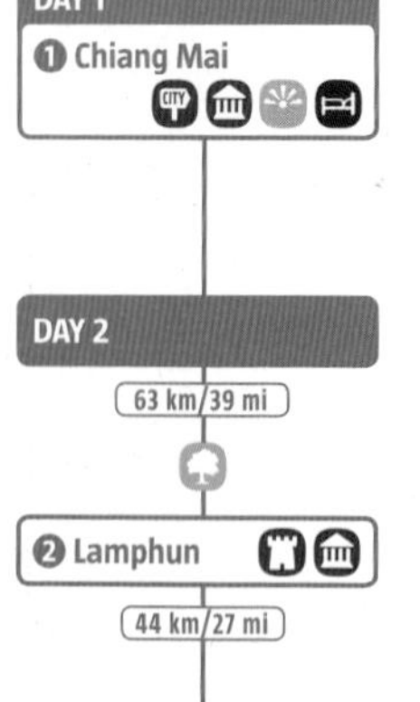

The starting point for this tour is **① Chiang Mai → p. 46**, where you will check into **The 3 Sis**. Visit the impressive temple buildings in the old city centre as well as the interesting history museums. Explore the **Wat Phra That Doi Suthep** situated beautifully above the city at your leisure.

On **Route 106 South**, you will drive through lovely avenues lined by old jungle trees, some of which have grown to a height of 40 m (130 ft), to get to **② Lamphun → p. 50**. The city was once the official residence of the rulers of the legendary kingdom of Haripunchai. The ruins of the old city walls and the beautiful **Wat Phra That Haripunchai** attest to its long history. **In less than a half hour's**

drive on Route 11 towards Lampang, you will come to the road that branches off to the ③ Thai Elephant Conservation Center *(daily 8am–3:30pm | www.thailandelephant.org)*. Watch one of the elephant shows *(200 baht)* and maybe even help wash one of the thick-skinned giants *(1,000 baht)*. You can also visit the elephant museum, kindergarten and hospital.

③ Thai Elephant Conservation Center

33 km/20 mi

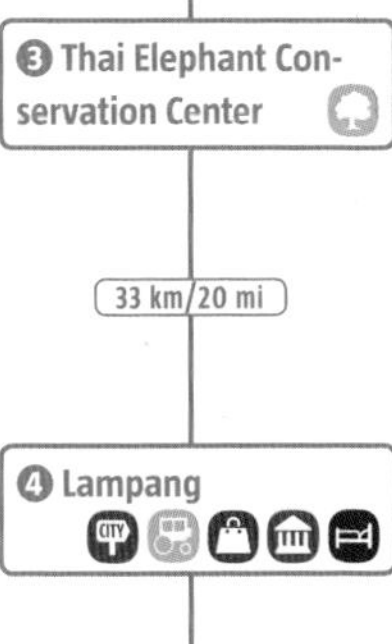

Return to Route 11 and drive to the busy, yet pleasant provincial capital of ④ Lampang (pop. 60,000). Hop onto one of the colourful horse-drawn carriages for a tour around the city *(200–300 baht)* and stop at some of the lively markets, stately temples and teak houses

④ Lampang

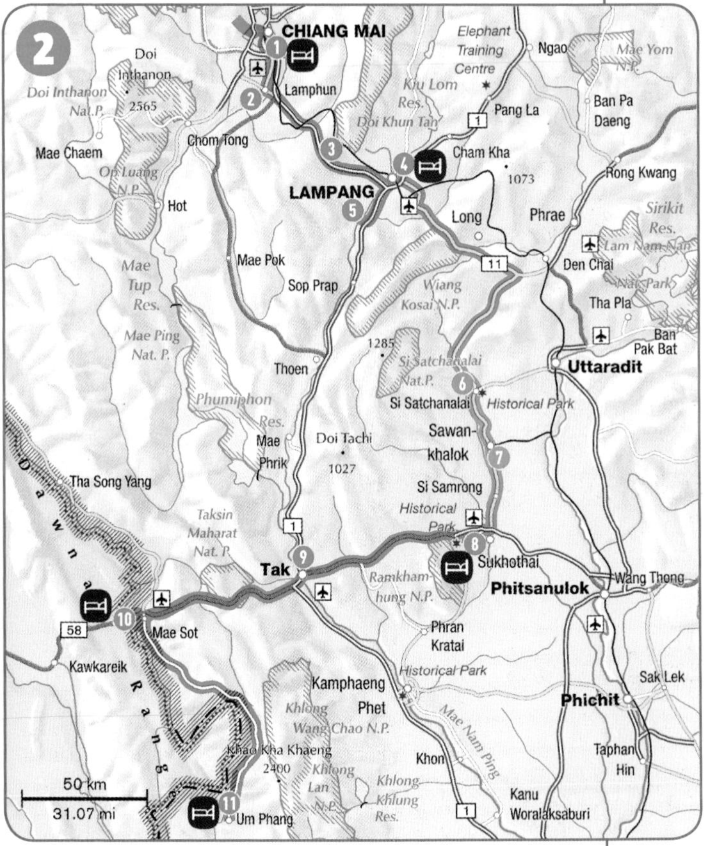

such as the **Baan Sao Nak** *(Ratwattana Rd | admission 50 baht)*. A special flair and personal service await you at **Auangkham Resort** *(14 rooms | 51 Wang Nua Rd | tel. 0 54 22 13 05 | www.auangkhamlampang.com | Budget)*. If you have time, make the worthwhile trip to 5 INSIDER TIP **Wat Phra That Lampang Luang** *(daily 7:30am–5pm | free admission)*, perhaps the most enthralling temple in northern Thailand. It is just a short journey to the southwest via **Route 1 and National Road 1034**.

On the third day, **Route 11 will lead you through rice paddies to the southeast to the junction with Route 101. Turn right towards Sukhothai.** At the historic park of 6 **Si Satchanalai** → p. 45, temple ruins tell the story of the city's past. **On the way, stop in Sawankhalok** to see the unique ceramic pieces at the 7 **Sawanworanayok National Museum** → p. 45. Continue on to 8 **Sukhothai** → p. 44. Not only does **Old Sukhothai** also have an impressive historical park, but also it is situated within an authentic rural setting. Explore the area on your fourth day on a guided mountain bike tour through the rice paddies and villages. The Frenchman Michel offers charming accommodation at **Lotus Village** and a warm Thai meal awaits in the popular restaurant **Rom Pho**.

Continue westward on Route 12 and look to the mountains in the distance. Several roads converge in Tak (pop. 25,000), which has little to offer other than the 9 **Statue of King Taksin** (1734–82) who was born here. There's no need to linger here, so **keep driving on the curvy Route 105 through the mountains to** 10 **Mae Sot** (pop. 55, 000) after a short break. Many of the shops glisten and shine because this multicultural city on the border to Myanmar is a centre of the gemstone trade. Visit the colourful **market at the end of Route 105, directly on the river Moei that marks the border to Myanmar.** For a simple, but clean and centrally-located accommodation, check into the **J2 Hotel** *(45 rooms | 149/8 Intarakeeree Rd | tel. 0 55 54 69 99 | Budget)*.

The next morning, it's time for the long drive **on National Road 1090** to the somewhat isolated 11 **Umphang** region. Spend the night at **Tu Ka Su Cottage** *(30 rooms | to the west of the bridge | tel. 0 55 56 12 95 | www.tukasu.webs.com | Budget)* and book a rafting or trekking tour for your last day on this route.

ADVENTURES IN THE JUNGLE OF THE GIGANTIC FLOWER

START: ① Phuket END: ① Phuket	3 days Driving time (without stops) 9 hours
Distance: 512 km/318 miles	

COSTS: approx. 270–300 euros for 2 people (rental car from 25 euros/day, petrol 32 euros, accommodation 50 euros/night, National Park admission 5 euros/day, jungle tours 12–17 euros, tubing 9 euros/hour and canoe tours 17 euros for 2 hours)
WHAT TO PACK: navigation system or smartphone with GPS, sun protection, mosquito repellent/nets, swim gear and a change of clothes

Together with the surrounding conservation areas, the Khao Sok National Park is the largest jungle area in southern Thailand. Explore this "evergreen" paradise on foot and by canoe.

DAY 1

① Phuket

As soon as you climb in the car and drive away from Phuket, there will be no doubt in your mind that this route is heading into the jungle – with a view of the blue ocean to boot. Leave **① Phuket** → p. 88 **on Route 402 North. At**

Hike through the jungle on the trails in Khao Sok National Park

the junction near the village of Khok Kloi, turn onto Route 4 and drive in the direction of Takua Pa. This area is only sparsely populated and the green jungle mountains spread almost to the sea. **Shortly before you come to Khao Lak**, you can enjoy the more than impressive view of the glimmering turquoise water. **Little roads branch off from the highway, leading to the beaches of** ❷ **Khao Lak** → p. 77. The road at kilometre-marker 60, for example, will take you to the lovely and broad **Nang Thong Beach**.

In Takua Pa, turn onto Route 401 heading towards Surat Thani. Take a moment to soak in the spectacular landscape with huge, rugged karst mountains that rise up almost vertically from the lush green jungle. Later in the afternoon, you will finally arrive at the entrance to ❸ ★ **Khao Sok National Park**. Surrounded by imposing limestone cliffs, the park is home to gigantic jungle trees whose buttress roots sometimes jut up over 2 metres tall (6.5 ft) and a large variety of animals. Sleep the next few nights in one of the romantic tree houses at INSIDER TIP **Our Jungle House** *(12 rooms | mobile tel. 08 14 17 05 46 | www.khaosokaccommodation.com | Budget–Moderate)*.

After a good night's sleep, head off into the park. It is easy to hike on your own if you **follow the marked trails**. The half-day jungle tours that you can book through the resorts and travel agencies also come well-recommended. The guides will lead you to waterfalls a bit further away and they know where to find the Rafflesia, which bear the largest flowers in the world. In the afternoon, head out on the water. Book a tubing excursion at your hotel and sail down the **Sok River** on your donut-shaped raft.

Begin the last day of this tour with a half-day canoe trip to the **Chiew Lan** reservoir with its steep limestone cliffs and enchanting caves. You can book this adventure tour at your hotel as well. Afterwards, it's time to hit the road again. **Drive west on Route 401, and turn left in Takua Pa onto National Road 4032. A bit**

to the south of the village, you will come across a real gem, namely the somewhat hidden ④ old town centre of Takua Pa → p. 79 where many aged Chinese storefronts still tell of the great era of the pewter boom in the 19th century. After a little stroll, get back in the car and **follow National Road 4032 and 4090 towards Phang Nga and then take Route 4 and Route 402 to return to ① Phuket → p. 88**.

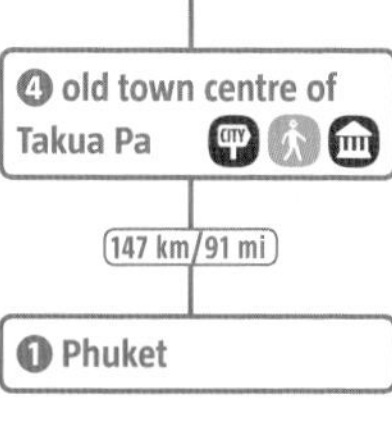

4 SUN, SAND AND FUN FOR THE WHOLE FAMILY

START: ① Bangkok END: ⑦ Trat	9 days Driving time (without stops) 12 hours
Distance: 640 km/400 miles	

COSTS: approx. 1,800 euros for a family of four (accommodation, food & drink, rental car, petrol, admission fees and excursions)
WHAT TO PACK: swim gear and sun protection

Thailand's east coast is perfect for a family-friendly tour with lots of variety using public transport. Start in Bangkok and follow along the 400-km long (250 miles) Sukhumvit Highway (Route 3) almost all the way to the border with Cambodia.

From ① **Bangkok** → p. 35, take a taxi **to the southeast on the Sukhumvit Highway** to get to the world's largest outdoor museum, ② **Ancient Siam** *(daily 9am–7pm | www.ancientcitygroup.net/ancientsiam)*. On a rental bike or a golf cart, you can explore "all of Thailand" in one day as replicas of over 100 attractions are dotted around the sprawling museum grounds. Afterwards, return to **your waiting taxi and take Route 3 directly to ③ Pattaya → p. 69**. The somewhat strange world of **Ripley's Believe It Or Not** is quite an experience for families with children. If you are interested in culture, head to the beautiful teak wood **Sanctuary of Truth**. The popular **Thai Garden Resort** is a good place to book a room for the night

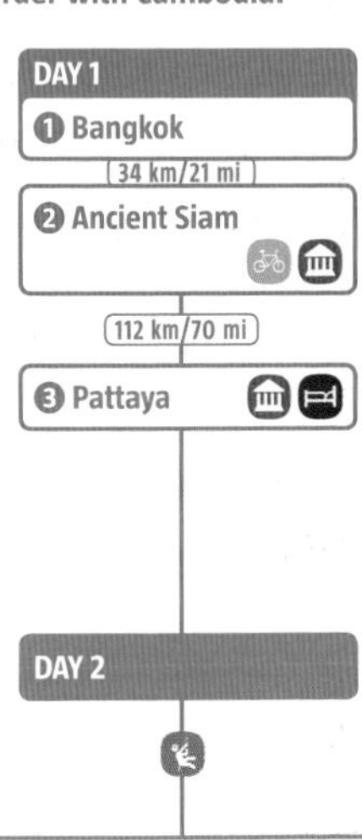

The next day is all about adventure with a zip line course. At **Flight of the Gibbon** *(www.treetopasia.com)*, you can

DAY 3–4

234 km/145 mi

4 Ko Samet

DAY 5

108 km/67 mi

5 Chantaburi

swing from tree to tree on steel cables. Once you have overcome your initial hesitation, you can enjoy a full adrenaline rush. A visit to the adjacent **Khao Kheow Open Zoo** is just the thing afterwards.

Your next destination is the island of 4 **Ko Samet** → p. 73. Spend two relaxing days at the pleasant **Vongduean Resort** situated directly on a fine sand beach. With the minibus from Malibu Travel *(tel. 038370259 | www.malibu-travel.com)*, **travel along the coast on Route 3 to Ban Phe, and cross over to the island with the resort's own ferry.** Just a ten minute walk from the resort will bring you to a INSIDER TIP fabulous place to watch the sunset. **Go through the entrance towards the street and follow the sunset signs to the cliffs on the other side of the island.**

Take the midday ferry back to the mainland and drive with a pre-chartered taxi along Route 3 to the charming town of 5 **Chantaburi** → p. 73, which is home to Thailand's largest cathedral, **Notre-Dame**. Don't miss out on the restaurant **Chanthorn Phochana** *(102/5–8 Benjamarachuthid Rd | tel. 039302350 | Budget)*, which dishes up the local speciality INSIDER TIP *Bai Cha Moung*, a tasty and rich herb soup. The town owes its wealth to its sapphire and ruby trade that is a quite profitable business at

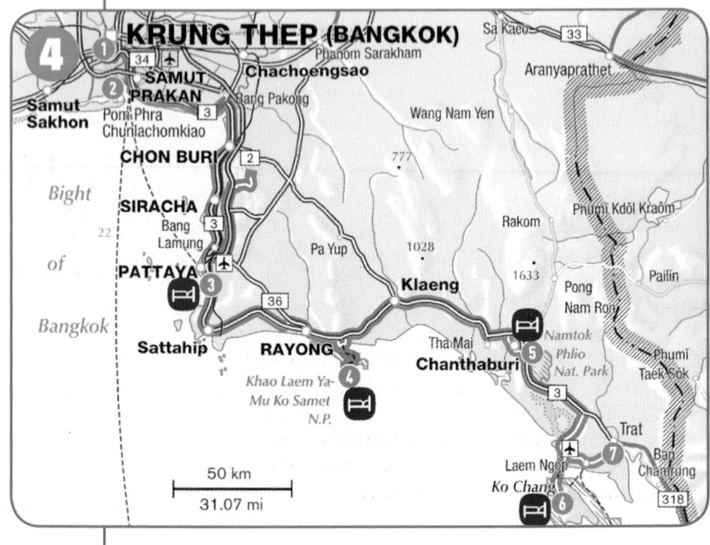

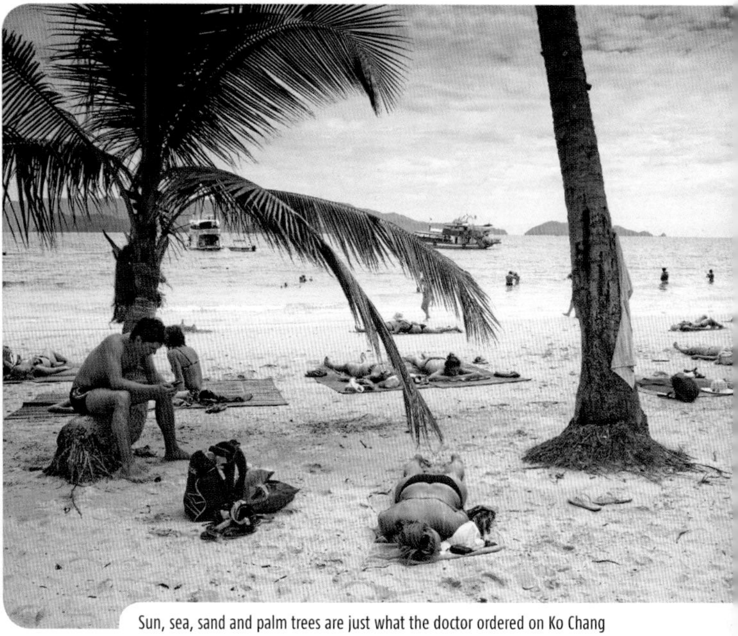

Sun, sea, sand and palm trees are just what the doctor ordered on Ko Chang

the moment. Visit the **Chantaburi Gem & Jewelry Center** *(daily 8am–7pm | Sri Chan Rd)* to admire the gemstones and jewellery. Book one of the comfortable, yet functional rooms at **Kasemsarn Hotel** *(60 rooms | 98/1 Benjamarachuthid Rd | tel. 0 39 31 23 40 | www.hotelkasemsarn.com | Budget)* for the night.

The next morning, take a **taxi along Route 3 and National Road 3156 to get to the ferry station Ao Thammachat near Trat. Ferries depart regularly for the hour-long trip to the island of ⑥ Ko Chang** **→ p. 64**. Settle into your room at **Klong Prao Resort** and hit the beach for a good dose of relaxing sun and sea. On the last two days on the island, gear up for a bit more activity. Book a kayak tour with Kayak Chang *(Klong Prao Beach | at Amari Emerald Cove Resort | www.kayakchang.com)* and a cruise through the archipelago with Thaifun Day-Cruise *(mobile tel. 08 10 03 48 00 | www.thaifun-kohchang.com)*. On your ninth day, **return to the mainland and take a taxi to ⑦ Trat** where you can catch a flight to Bangkok.

SPORTS & ACTIVITIES

Not content just to lie on the beach? Then take tgo for a dive, climb, or ride. Are you looking for relaxation? Give your mind a rest while practicing yoga, or treat yourself to a Thai massage.

BALLOON RIDES

Want to experience Thailand from above? No problem: you'll find information on hot air balloon rides at *www.balloonadventurethailand.com/index.*

DIVING

The best dive sites are located in the Andaman Sea in the waters around Phuket and Khao Lak; the uninhabited ★ *Similan Islands* 50 km (31 miles) west of Khao Lak rank among the world's top diving destinations, but also around the Phi Phi Islands and down the coast to the Malaysian border a colourful underwater world awaits the diver. The premier dive sites in the Gulf of Thailand are around the small island Ko Tao north of Ko Samui, but there are also great sites off Pattaya and Ko Chang. A one-day excursion with two dives costs approx. 3,100 baht; a three- to four-day basic course starts at 7,800 baht. For detailed information on dive sites, seasons, etc, visit: *www.divetheworldthailand.com*

GOLF

Golf courses are plentiful in Thailand. Top destinations are Pattaya with

From trekking and diving to massages and yoga – Thailand offers everything from thrilling adventures to relaxing spa days

around a dozen courses and Phuket with seven courses of international standard, but there are also great courses in Bangkok, Kanchanaburi, Chiang Mai, Hua Hin, at Khao Yai National Park and on Ko Samui. You can request a golf brochure from the Tourism Authority of Thailand. Interesting websites for golf buffs *www.golforient.com, www.thailandgolfcourse.com, www.kanchanaburi.com/golf.html, www.thaigolfer.com, www.golfpattaya.com, www.huahingolf.com, www.golfhuahin.com, www.samui.sawadee.com/golf, www.phuket-golf.com*

HORSE TREKKING

Boris Mimietz and his attentive team at the *Thai Horse Farm (Phrao | 100 km (62 miles) north of Chiang Mai | mobile tel. 08 69 19 38 46 | www.thaihorsefarm.com)* will lead you through the Sri Lanna National Park atop Asian mountain horses. The tours in small groups are suitable for beginners who have never before sat on a horse, making for a stress-free adventure off the beaten tourist track. For a one-day tour including room & board plus transport to and from Chiang Mai as well as all the necessary equipment, you will pay approx 7,000 baht; four nights cost 26,000 baht.

MASSAGES & WELLBEING

There is definitely a reason why Thailand is one of the most famous spa destinations. From exclusive spas in the luxury hotels of the South and the chrome palaces of Bangkok to the cheap and ubiquitous massage salons in the cities, the women offering massages on the beach, and the traditional healers in the villages of the northeast, massages have a strong tradition and an equally promising future in Thailand. Simple treatments run from just150 baht per hour, but you can easily spend four times as much. Thai-style massages are known for their focus on the Ayurvedic pressure points and their intense flexing and stretching positions. For some tourists, the strong pressure applied with knees, feet, elbows and the balls of hands is too painful. You will doubtlessly be surprised at the strength of an experienced masseuse. If you would like to learn how to practise this ancient craft yourself, *the Massage School at the Wat Pho* (see p. 37) in Bangkok or the *International Training Massage School (tel. 0 53 21 86 32 | www.itmthaimassage.com)* in Chiang Mai are good addresses.

ROCK CLIMBING

Rock climbers from all over the world test their skills on the bolted limestone cliffs at the beaches of Railay and Ton Sai in Krabi and are rewarded with spectacular views over the coast and the sea. Chiang Mai also has some good climbs. Introductory course 780–1,200 baht. *www.railay.com, www.thailandclimbing.com, www.rockclimbing-thailand.info, www.thepeakadventure.com*

SAILING

With its beautiful islands, the Andaman Sea is an eldorado for sailors. But you can also set sail in the Gulf of Thailand (Pattaya, Ko Chang, Ko Samui). The list of charter companies in Thailand is virtually endless. *www.phuket.net/things-to-do/sailing, www.yachtcharterguide.com, www.yachtcharterthailand.com, www.phuket.com/sailing*

SEA CANOE TOURS

The limestone cliffs of Phang Nga Bay provide a stunning backdrop for a canoeing trip. There are day trips from Phuket from around 3,900 baht as well as tours lasting three days with overnight stays on the accompanying boat or in tents on the beach for around 27,000 baht. Holidaymakers on Ko Samui can paddle through the islands of the National Maritime Park, Ang Thong.

Phuket: *John Gray's Sea Canoe (tel. 0 76 25 45 05 | www.johngray-seacanoe.com)*

Ko Samui: *Blue Stars Sea Kayaking (tel. 0 77 30 06 15 | www.bluestars.info)*

Krabi: *Tha Lane Bay Discovery (mobile tel. 0 8 88 25 35 34 | www.aonangkrabithailand.com*

Bookings can also be made through local travel agencies.

TREKKING

Hiking through the forested mountains of the North is a fantastic experience. But even more interesting for many tourists is the chance to come into contact with the mountain tribes that cling to their traditions in isolated villages. The centre of trekking tourism is Chiang Mai, but from there it's several hours drive before you get into any real mountains. If you start your ★ trekking adventure in Pai or in Mae Hong Son, you are already among the mountains. Most tours also include an elephant ride and bamboo rafting. A three-day tour for six people will cost around 1,500 baht each. It's advisable to use only travel agencies that are registered with the Tourism Authority of Thailand. Information on trekking and all national parks is available at: *www.trekthailand.net* and *www.dnp.go.th.*

WHITE-WATER RAFTING

The INSIDER TIP Umphang Jungle, 170 km (105 miles) south of Mae Sot in the Thailand/Myanmar border region, is considered the most virgin area of tropical rainforest in the country. The Mae Klong River winds its way through the wilderness, sometimes at a leisurely pace, sometimes churning over rapids and waterfalls. Several operators in Mae Sot and Umphang offer rafting tours, e.g. *Max One Tour (296/2 Intarakeeree Rd | Mae Sot | tel. 055542942 | www.maxonetour.com).* A four-day tour (min. 2 people) costs approx. 12,000 baht per person. Adventurous rafting tours are also offered on the Pai River near the town of Pai from June to January.

YOGA

A vacation for body and soul: yoga and meditation are offered at several retreats. The island of ● *Ko Phangan* in particular has developed as a spiritual centre for those who want to explore their inner selves. Addresses and links: *www.yoga-centers-directory.net/thailand.htm* and *www.thaiwebsites.com/yoga.asp.*

Trekking tour near Mae Hong Son

TRAVEL WITH KIDS

Travellers with children are warmly welcomed everywhere. Don't be surprised to see Thais pat your children on the head or take them by the hand.

The joy Thais display towards children of *farang* is genuine. Even in smaller hotels and resorts, little guests are often treated like family, and staff may occasionally even volunteer to fill in as a babysitters. Economically-priced rooms in particular are often furnished with three beds or a double and a single bed; an additional bed or mattress can be supplied on request.

You can buy baby food and nappies at supermarkets in the tourist centres and larger towns. It's advisable to leave your buggy at home though: pavements – if there are any – are not usually in the best state of repair, and progress can be torture, especially if they're blocked by souvenir stalls. A more practical option is a baby or child carrier for your back or chest. Once you're at the beach, however, the little ones can run freely and there is always something to discover. And there are attractions aplenty to delight children besides the sand and the sea.

CENTRAL THAILAND

BANGKOK DOLL MUSEUM

(U E3) (*🕮 e3*)

The exotic dolls in the Bangkok Doll Museum are beautifully handcrafted with meticulous attention to detail. The costumed hill tribe figures are particularly colourful. The small works of art are also

A kingdom for kids: children are welcome in Thailand. And exciting adventures are around every corner

for sale. *Mon–Sat 8:30am–5pm | free admission | 85 Soi Ratchataphan | side street at Ratchaprarop Rd | Bangkok | www.bangkokdolls.com*

DREAM WORLD

(131 D5) (*🕮 D9*)

A huge theme park featuring a nostalgic train, Wonderful Garden, Fairy Tale Land, *Snow World* and many more rides and shows. *Mon–Fri 10am–5pm, Sat, Sun 10am–7pm | admission 550 baht (without Snow World and Go-carts), free for children shorter than 90 cm | Tour from Bangkok incl. lunch 1,200 baht | 62 Rangsit-Ongkarak Rd | Rangsit | approx. 10 minutes' drive north of the Don Muang Airport | www.dreamworld-th/en*

KIDZANIA BANGKOK

(U D4) (*🕮 d4*)

A miniature city planned down to the last detail where kids can try out all kids of jobs and professions. Among the more than 80 different choices, there are dream jobs such as firefighter, pilot or doctor as well as more unusual ones including sushi chef, secret agent or forensics expert. Everything is sponsored by big-name companies, which means that little mechanics work on Toyota cars and Coca-Cola bottles have to be filled. *Mon–Fri 10am–5pm, Sat, Sun 10:30am–8:30pm | admission Mon–Fri 425 baht, children 850 baht, Sat, Sun 500 baht, children 1,000 baht | 991 Rama I Rd | Siam Paragon | 5th floor | Bangkok | bangkok.kidzania.com*

MADAME TUSSAUDS

(U D4) *(🕮 d4)*

At this offshoot of the world-famous wax museum, kids can look celebrities such as Katy Perry, Beyoncé, Brad Pitt, Spiderman and Cristiano Ronaldo in the eye. *Daily 10am–8pm | admission 850 baht, children 650 baht | 989 Rama I Rd | Siam Discovery Center | 6th floor | Bangkok | www.madametussauds.com/bangkok*

SEA LIFE BANGKOK OCEAN WORLD

(U D4) *(🕮 d4)*

Coral fish, manta rays and even penguins call Thailand's largest aquarium home. Kids will be delighted when they walk under the glass tunnel in the middle of the shark tank or through the life-like rain forest. *Daily 10am–8pm | admission 990 baht, children 790 baht | 991 Rama I Rd | in the Siam Paragon shopping centre | Bangkok | www.sealifebangkok.com/en*

THE NORTH

CHIANG MAI ZOO

(126 C3) *(🕮 B3)*

The stars of this extensive zoo are two pandas, a gift from the Chinese government. But in Thailand's largest zoo, there are over 400 other species such as Thai elephants, African giraffes and Australian koala bears. Watch the sharks and small fish at theadjacent aquarium. In the *Snow Dome* visitors both large and small can even go sledging on the artificial snow. *Daily 8am–5pm | admission 150 baht, children 70 baht (100/50 baht extra for the panda zone, 150 baht for the Snow Dome) | 100 Huay Kaew Rd | Chiang Mai | www.chiangmaizoo.com*

ELEPHANT CAMPS

(126 C2–3) *(🕮 B3)*

Near Chiang Mai there are several so-called elephant camps. The pachyderms are trained to stack logs, stand on their hind legs, play football and even paint. They also take visitors on rides around the camp. The best-known camps are *Chiang Dao (www.chiangdaoelephantcamp.com)* on Hwy. 107 north of Chiang Mai, and *Mae Sa Elephant Camp (www.maesaelephantcamp.com)* on Hwy. 1096 northwest of Chiang Mai.

LOVE ANIMAL HOUSE

(126 C3) *(🕮 B3)*

Over 100 abandoned animals are cared for at this facility, whose work is supported by members and donations. The *Bearhugs Club* is dedicated to the black bear "Teddy". The Love Animal House also organises children's birthday parties and family weekends around the campfire. It is necessary to book in advance. *Admission (donation) 200 baht | Mae Rim | approx. 20 km north of Chiang Mai | Tel. 0 98 55 59 23 | www.animal-sanctuary.chiangmai-chiangrai.com*

EAST COAST

KHAO KHEOW OPEN ZOO ★

(134 D2) *(🕮 D10)*

This lush animal sanctuary, which operates under the patronage of the royal family, is internationally recognised for its animal management and operations.

Around 8,000 animals from hippos and lions to orang-utans live as close to their natural habitat as possible in the expansive jungle park. Night safaris are also organized. In the *Children's Zoo,* numerous baby animals await visitors. *Daily 9am–5pm, night safari 7pm | several tours on offer, also with overnight stay, incl. pickup service from Bangkok or Pattaya | approx. 50 km (31 miles) north of Pattaya | www.kkopenzoo.com | www.journeytothejungle.com*

THE SOUTH

DINO PARK

(136 C6) (🗺 A–B16)

For dinosaur fans: This mini golf course features an artificial volcano and encounters with a variety of dinosaur species. As you go round, it's easy to imagine yourself being back in prehistoric times. *Daily 10am–midnight (the volcano glows only when it is dark) | admission 240 baht, children 180 baht | Karon Beach | Phuket | www.dinopark.com*

PARADISE PARK FARM

(137 E3) (🗺 C14))

A large park with goats, rabbits, ponies – a giant petting zoo located in the hills above Ko Samui's west coast. It also features a restaurant, pool, terrific view of the coast, and pleasant temperatures. *Daily 8:30am–5pm | admission 300 baht, children 100 baht | pick-up service available | junction of the ring road at the village of Ban Saket (signposted) | www.paradiseparkfarm.com*

In the kingdom of Thailand, the smallest are the greatest

SIAM SAFARI *(136 C6) (🗺 B16)*

Whether you're in the mood for an elephant ride, kayak tour or jungle safari: this award-winning organisation has a packed programme to impress big and small travellers alike. The *Siam Safari Elephant Project* supports regular health checks for elephants in Phuket and forwards donations to the elephant hospital in the North Thai city of Lampang. *Chao Fa Rd | Chalong (on the road to the airport) | Phuket | www.siamsafari.com*

FESTIVALS & EVENTS

The timing of religious festivals depends on the position of the sun and the moon, so dates vary from year to year. Local festivals can be similarly moveable. The state tourism authority TAT (www.tourismthailand.org) compiles festival dates every year. You can also find a good summary at: *www.thaifestivalblogs.com.* The Buddhist calendar begins with the birth of The Enlightened One. The year 2016 A.D. corresponds to the year 2559 after Buddha.

HOLIDAYS & FESTIVALS

JANUARY

Bor Sang Umbrella Festival: The village of Bor Sang near Chiang Mai in Northern Thailand is renowned for its hand-painted paper umbrellas. On a parade, girls in festive costumes present the most beautiful umbrellas.

JANUARY/FEBRUARY

Chinese New Year: New Year in Bangkok's Chinatown and in many other cities is ushered in with a procession of Chinese deities accompanied by colourful lion and dragon dancing. In Phuket a one-week Temple Festival takes place in the monastery of Wat Chalong (by the village of Chalong).

FEBRUAR

Flower Festival: This three-day long colourful fair with a large flower show takes place on the first weekend in February in Chiang Mai. The highlight is the breathtaking parade on Saturday featuring floats artfully decorated with flowers, people in traditional dress and lots of music.

APRIL

★ ● ***Songkran*** *(www.songkran.net):* Thai New Year (13–15 April) is the wildest festival of all, celebrated by throwing water at everybody in sight. Tourists are not exempt. Some of the biggest celebrations (with a big parade) are in Chiang Mai, where festivities actually begin a day early, on 12 April. In Bangkok, the centre of the water fights is the Khao San Road.

MAY

★ ***Royal Ploughing Ceremony Day:*** Held during the second week in May, this festival marks the beginning of the rice planting season. A colourful procession takes place at the Grand Palace in Bangkok with the royal family in attendance. Grandstand seats can be booked at tourist offices in Bangkok.

SEPTEMBER/OCTOBER

Buffalo racing: Farm hands are the jockeys and water buffaloes are the mounts for this race meeting in Chonburi (between Bangkok and Pattaya).

★ ***Vegetarian festival*** *(www.phuketvegetarian.com):* Bizarre festival in Phuket and, on a smaller scale, in Trang (Southern Thailand). Ethnic Chinese Thais work themselves into a trance before skewering needles, hooks, knives and even drills or umbrellas though their flesh. The participants adhere to a strict vegetarian diet during the festival.

NOVEMBER

★ ***Loi Kratong:*** The most enchanting festival of the year takes place at full moon in November. Baskets with flowers, incense and burning candles are floated in the water. The most romantic festivities take place in Sukhothai and Ayutthaya as well as in Chiang Mai.

NOVEMBER/DECEMBER

River Kwai Bridge Week: The famous Bridge on the River Kwai and the "Death Railway" are the venues for this festival at Kanchanaburi, featuring rides on old steam trains and impressive firework displays with light and sound shows on the bridge.

NATIONAL HOLIDAYS

1 Jan	New Year's Day
full moon in March	Buddha's teaching in front of 1,250 believers
6 April	Rama I's accession to the throne
13–15 April	*Songkran* (Thai New Year))
1 May	Labour Day
5 May	Coronation day of King Bhumiboll
full moon in May	Buddha's birth, enlightenment and death
full moon in July	Buddha's first sermon
day after full moon in July	Start of Buddhist Lent
12 Aug	Birthday of Queen Sirikit
23 Oct	Death of King Chulalongkorn
5 Dec	Birthday of King Bhumibol
10 Dec	Constitution Day
31 Dec	New Year's Eve

LINKS, BLOGS, APPS & MORE

LINKS & BLOGS

bk.asia-city.com Comprehensive on-line magazine (updated daily) for Bangkok featuring event announcements, restaurant reviews and tips for day trips and nights out on the town

www.bangkokadvisor.com/Bangkok-Food-and-Drink.htm Simply reading about Thai food will make your mouth water. A street list revealing the best Thai restaurants

www.travelfish.org Specialises in inexpensive accommodation. Cheeky descriptions, praise, as well as criticism. The coolest site for budget travellers on the worldwide web

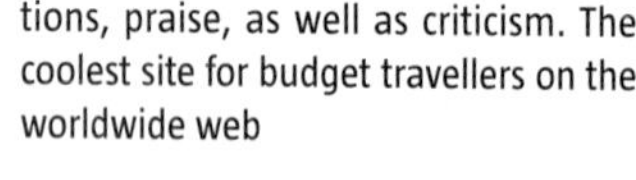

www.thailandqa.com The abbreviation *qa* stands for question and answer. Here's where you'll find questions and answers about life and travel in Thailand

www.amazing-thailand.com Everything at a glance for your holiday destination: facts, general info, travel,...

www.thaivisa.com/forum/ Where is a good place to go for breakfast in Hua Hin? Who provides bicycle tours in Bangkok? If you have questions, this well-attended forum will have an already blogged answer

www.thai-blogs.com Thailand's most famous blogger leaves no stone unturned. Richard Barrow writes on anything ranging from the fast-food kiosks on the street to the „cigarette police" who rip off tourists

www.thailand-uk.com/forums Whether you're curious about politics or culture, hotel ratings or visa regulations, this forum has the information you need.

www.couchsurfing.org Hospitality in the land of smiles: Thais and foreigners who live in Thailand use this site for offering a couch or bed for a night

Regardless of whether you are still preparing your trip or already in Thailand: these addresses will provide you with more information, videos and networks to make your holiday even more enjoyable.

www.hospitalityclub.org The club is "a worldwide web of friendly people". Over 1,000 members in Thailand alone are registered. You can stay overnight – for free – with registered members, get valuable tips or even take a walk around the block

www.thaizer.com Roy Cavanagh lives in Thailand and knows everything about the country and its people. Useful advice on dos and don'ts, health, transport, the language and much more. Blog which is updated regularly.

http://uleven.com/funniest-thailand-advertisement-1/ Thai commercials are often bizarre and laugh-out-loud funny. Observe the advertising gimmicks businesses use to attract customers in the land of smiles

VIDEOS

http://www.tripfilms.com/Tourism-l764-Thailand-Travel_Videos.html Video clips of many destinations throughout the country, covering just about everything from hotels and palaces to dive sites!

https://www.youtube.com/channel/UC7ohHG5zM5V7y-l7Eyqoisg/videos Two travel bloggers take you along on their adventures in Thailand to places like Ko Chang, Chiang Mai and Bangkok

APPS

Amazing Thailand App with information on the most significant tourist destinations and lovely pictures, but unfortunately the practical tips are often a bit outdated

Green Tourism A guide to eco-friendly travel destinations and resorts put together by the Tourism Authority of Thailand.

Learn Thai – Phrasebook An easy-to-use language app with the most important conversation building blocks, which you can also play out loud

Wongnai Thais love food! This popular app makes it easy to find the right restaurant every time and eat where the locals love to go

The Publisher shall not be held responsible for the contents of the links, blogs, apps, etc. listed here

TRAVEL TIPS

ACCOMMODATION

The categories provided in this edition for hotel prices apply to the standard high season from around mid-November to the end of February. Many hotels add an additional surcharge of 10 to 20 percent for the peak season between Christmas and New Year. During off-season expect a discount. Booking over the Internet, either from the hotel website or via websites offering specialised hotel bookings is often cheaper. Hotel rooms in Thailand are always double rooms and you pay the same price even if you are travelling solo. Last-minute deals: *www.latestays.com.* Not only of interest to backpackers: *www.travelfish.org.* Experience shows that room rates for package tours (flight and accommodation) are significantly lower than by booking directly. It's worth doing a comparison.

Unfortunately, in Thailand it is a common practice for hotels to foist a compulsory, expensive dinner on their guests over Christmas and New Year. Make sure to check booking details prior to your arrival to avoid an unpleasant surprise.

RESPONSIBLE TRAVEL

It doesn't take a lot to be environmentally friendly whilst travelling. Don't just think about your carbon footprint whilst flying to and from your holiday destination but also about how you can protect nature and culture abroad. As a tourist it is especially important to respect nature, look out for local products, cycle instead of driving, save water and much more. If you would like to find out more about eco-tourism please visit: *www.ecotourism.org*

ARRIVAL

Bangkok's Suvarnabhumi airport (pronounced: *Suwannapum / www.suvarnabhumiairport.com)* is a hub for Southeast Asia and is served by most European and Asian airlines. The flight from London is approx. 11 hours. Charter airlines also land on the island of Phuket *(www.phuketairportthai.com/en).* Even during the December/January high season non-stop return flights from London to Bangkok with major airlines such British Airways or Thai Airways are available for around £ 900 (US-$ 1,420); cheap return flights to Bangkok or Phuket with one stopover can be had for as little as £ 400 (US-$ 630). Shortly before Christmas, however, the prices sometimes spike. You'll find cheap flights at *www.flightcentre.co.uk; www.cheapticket.co.uk; www.cheapflights.co.uk; www.travelsupermarket.com; www.southalltravel.co.uk* and many other Internet agencies, but it's also worth contacting airlines such as Qatar Airways direct.

The cheapest means of transport from the Bangkok and Phuket airports into the city and to the beaches are train (Bangkok, *www.bangkokairporttrain.com*), bus or *Meter Taxi*. A trip by *Meter Taxi* from Bangkok Airport to the lower Sukhumvit Rd costs approx. 300 baht, and from Phuket Airport to Patong Beach around 800 baht.

BANKING & CREDIT CARDS

Travellers' cheques in dollars, pounds and euros are accepted at all banks (Mon–Fri

8:30am–3:30pm; exchange counter daily, often until 10pm). It's much easier to use a credit/debit card at an ATM, available outside banks in all towns, cities and tourist centres. Visa is accepted by all large banks; Mastercard/Eurocard is also widespread. With an American Express Card, you'll only get cash at the branches of the *Bangkok Bank*. All banks charge a fee of 180 baht per transaction for money withdrawals. If you lose your bankcard, call your home branch immediately to have it stopped. Always have the UK telephone number of your card provider on hand. Many shops accept credit cards, but they tend to add a hefty surcharge for the service. Tip: if you pay by cash, you can often negotiate a lower price.

CAR HIRE & DRIVING

Several local and international companies rent vehicles, such as *Avis (www.avisthailand.com)* and *Budget Rent A Car (www.budget.co.th)*. A small car costs approx. 1,200 baht per day (discount available for longer rental periods). Make sure your insurance includes personal and property damage waivers. An international driver's licence is mandatory. Driving is on the left, as in the UK. The speed limit on motorways is 120 km/h, but just 90 km/h on highways and national roads. The blood alcohol limit is 0.5 per mille. It can't be said enough that those who chose to drive themselves should drive defensively and refrain from insisting on the right of way. Watch out for the often risky and aggressive driving style of the locals. An alternative: a rental vehicle with a driver (for an eight-hour day for an extra charge of only 600 baht is common).

CHILD PROTECTION

Do you have compassion? Do you buy flowers, chewing gum or cigarettes from children to show your generosity? The child protection organisation *Childwatch Phuket (www.childwatchphuket.org)* strongly advises against it: "The more people that buy from the children, the stronger the likelihood they will have to work early the next morning." Children do not work at night in bar districts out of pure necessity; child labour is a highly organised business run by ruthless people.

CLIMATE, WHEN TO GO

In the "cool" seasons from November to February daily temperatures average 30°C, lower in the north. From March until May

BUDGETING

Noodle soup	23–47 baht *for a bowl from the cook shop*
T-Shirt	120–200 baht *for a shirt from a street vendor*
Drinking water	10–23 baht *for a bottle (1 litre) from the supermarket*
Beer	40–120 baht *for a bottle (0.3 l) at a restaurant*
Petrol	32 baht *for a litre of super*
Massage	353 baht *for a one-hour massage on the beach*

it can get as hot as 40°C/104°F. During the rainy season brought by the southwest monsoon from May to October temperatures abate somewhat, but the humidity increases. The sea is at its calmest from December/January to March/April. Ko Samui feels the effects of the northeast monsoon from November/December to the middle of February. But because mountains protect Thailand's eastern coast, the island is rarely troubled by the southwest monsoon coming down from India. So the European spring to autumn is a good season to travel to the islands in the Gulf of Thailand. Keep in mind that swimming in the ocean during the monsoon seasons can be fatal! The tourist industry markets the rainy season as the "Green Season" and offers good deals at this time of year, but this is not the time to plan a trip if you want to hit the beach.

CURFEW

The nightly curfew is set by the government at 1am, for selected nightlife districts at 2am.

CUSTOMS

No customs duties apply to items for personal use brought into the country. Foreign exchange in excess of 10,000 US dollars must be declared. Importing of illegal drugs, firearms and pornographic media is forbidden. Antiques, art and Buddha images acquired in Thailand require an export licence before they are taken out of the country. Numerous animal products and antique Buddha statues cannot be taken out at all.

DOMESTIC FLIGHTS

You can fly cheaply from Bangkok to nearly every major provincial city in Thailand. A flight to Phuket with Thai Airways *(www.thaiair.com)* costs from approx. 3,900 baht. Air Asia *(www.airasia.com)*, Bangkok Airways *(www.bangkokair.com)* and Nok Air *(www.nokair.com)* or Thai Lion Air *(www.lionairthai.com)* will fly you to your holiday destination often for just over half that price. It is definitely worthwile to compare prices.

ELECTRICITY

The supply voltage is 220 volts. In the province, some places still use plugs with flat prongs. You can purchase an adaptor at electrical stores.

EMBASSIES

UK EMBASSY

14 Wireless Rd | Lumpini, Pathumwan | Bangkok 10330 | tel. 0 23 05 83 33 | www.ukinthailand.fco.gov.uk | Mon–Thu 8–noon and 12:45–4:30; Fri 8–1 pm

US EMBASSY

American Citizen Services | U.S. Embassy | 95 Wireless Rd | Bangkok 10330 | tel. 0 22 05 40 49 | www.bangkok.usembassy.gov | Mon–Fri 7:30–11am and 1–2 pm

HEALTH

Vaccinations are not mandatory. In jungle regions near Myanmar and Cambodia there is a low but significant risk of malaria, which should not put yoou off a trekking tour. Information about malaria malaria prophylaxis: Department of Health *(www.dh.gov.uk)*; National Travel Health Network and Centre *(www.nathnac.org)*; Malaria Reference Laboratory (MRL) *(www.malaria-reference.co.uk)*. Engaging in unprotected sex puts you at considerable risk of contracting a sexually transmitted disease or becoming infected with HIV. Tap water is not safe to drink, but can be used for brushing your teeth. The standard of hygiene in Thailand is generally good. Additional health tips are available at the above websites.

Many doctors and dentists practising in Bangkok and tourist centres will have been trained in Europe or America. Private hospitals in particular may well have better standards of service, and at a cheaper price, than in the West. Renowned clinics in Bangkok are the *Bumrungrad Hospital (tel. 0 26 67 10 00 | www.bumrungrad.com)* and the *BNH Hospital (tel. 0 26 86 27 00 | www.bnhhospital.com;* in Chiang Mai the *Chiang Mai Ram Hospital (tel. 0 53 92 03 00 | www.chiangmairam.com);* in Pattaya the *Bangkok Pattaya Hospital (tel. 0 38 25 99 99 | www.bph.co.th);* and in Phuket the *Bangkok Phuket Hospital (tel. 0 76 25 44 25 | www.phuket hospital.com).* Smaller clinics in Ko Samui are *Bangkok Hospital Samui (tel. 0 77 42 95 00 | www.samuihospital.com)* and at Ko Chang the *Bangkok Trat Hospital (tel. 0 39 53 27 35 | www.bangkok trathospital.com).* All hospitals provide 24-hour emergency services. Most Thai hospitals also offer outpatient care. As there is no national system for emergency medical assistance, you have to call the hospitals directly and request ambulance service. The hospitals will contact your insurance carrier directly to determine whether they will cover the costs, which means that you should always carry your insurance card with you. If your insurance carrier does not guarantee payment immediately, you will have to pay the bill yourself first. If you insurance policy does not cover Thailand or you are planning a longer stay, it is a good idea to book travel health insurance.

Many independent doctors and dentists also provide a high standard of care. A professional teeth cleaning, for example, can be had for approx. 780 baht. Eyeglasses and medications are also very inexpensive, and most are available without a prescription.

CURRENCY CONVERTER

£	THB	THB	£
1	53	10	0.19
3	159	30	0.56
5	266	50	0.94
13	690	130	2.45
40	2,125	400	7.53
75	3,985	750	14.12
120	6,375	1,200	22.59
250	13,280	2,500	47.06
500	26,560	5,000	94.12

$	THB	THB	$
1	36	10	0.28
3	108	30	0.83
5	180	50	1.39
13	469	130	3.61
40	1,441	400	11.10
75	2,703	750	20.81
120	4,325	1,200	33.30
250	9,010	2,500	69.37
500	18,020	5,000	138.73

For current exchange rates see www.xe.com

IMMIGRATION

For a visit not exceeding 30 days, visitors from many countries, including the UK, do not need a visa to enter Thailand, just a passport valid for at least 6 months, and a return or onward ticket. Visas can usually be extended by up to 10 days at immigration offices throughout the country. If you plan to stay more than a month, obtain a 60-day visa at a Thai consulate or embassy in your country before leaving home. Check *(www.thaivisa.com)* or the websites of Thailand's immigration *(www.immigration.go.th)* and the Ministry of Foreign Affairs *(www.mfa.go.th)* for details.

DIPLOMATIC REPRESENTATION

UK: *Royal Thai Embassy in London | 29–30 Queen's Gate | London SW7 5JB | tel. 030 794810 | www.thaiembassyuk.org.uk*

US: *Royal Thai Embassy in Washington | 1024 Wisconsin Ave. | N.W. Washington D.C. 20007 | tel. 202 9443600 | www.thaiembdc.org*

INTERNET ACCESS & WIFI

Internet cafés are becoming a rarity in thailand, but they are cheap (about 20 baht per hour for access). In many restaurants, cafés, bars and hotels, you can go online via WiFi with our own device. Obtaining the password is sometimes very expensive in big hotels; most of the time it is now free. It is definitely easier and cheaper to use your own smartphone with a Thai SIM card to go on-line. You can easily buy one in shops or at any 7-eleven mini market.

MEDIA

The English-language dailies "Bangkok Post" *(www.bangkokpost.com)* and "The Nation" *(www.nationmultimedia.com)* are available at most hotels and airports as well as newsstands. Free English-language weekly "BK Magazine" *(http://bk.asia-city.com)* and monthly "Bangkok 101" have good listings and reviews of sights, restaurants and happenings in the capital. The tourist centres carry leading foreign newspapers and magazines.

There are five terrestrial Bangkok TV channels, and many programmes are foreign shows, mostly American, which are dubbed into Thai. Most leading hotels provide satellite TV channels, which usually include CNN, CNBC and BBC.

MOTORCYCLES

The mountains of the north with their curvy roads and slopes are both a challenge and an unforgettable experience for bikers. For everything you need to know about motorcycle tours in this area, check out *www.gt-rider-com.*

PHONE & MOBILE PHONE

The dialling code for the UK is 00144, for the US 001, for Australia 0061; dial the local area code without the zero. The international dialling code for Thailand is 0066; then dial the local number without the zero. In Thailand the area code must be dialled even for local calls: these are the first two (Bangkok) or first three (province) digits of the telephone numbers given in this guide.

If you bring your own mobile phone, the Thai mobile phone company automatically dials the network for your home company. The roaming fees, however, are steep, and you'll also have to pay the bulk of the fees for incoming overseas calls. A more economical option is to telephone with a Thailand SIM card, for which you will receive your own telephone number (you need to ensure your phone is unlocked). These top-up cards are available at various shops including all *7-Eleven stores*. You will only have to register once with your passport. Calling direct to the UK or USA from your mobile phone can be expensive, but the Thai mobile phone companies offer calling cards and prefixes with much better rates. With True Move (truemoveh.truecorp.co.th), you can call home to the UK for just 1 baht per minute to a landline or 6 baht per minute to a mobile. A call to the USA costs just 1 baht per minute to a landline or a mobile phone. Other major companies include AIS *(www.ais.co.th)* and DTAC *(www.dtac.co.th)*. It is also free to call from Skype to Skype from an Internet café or from your own Laptop.

If you're looking for a second mobile phone to accommodate a Thai SIM card, you're in luck, since they are available at many stores. A brand new mobile phone without bells and whistles and a contract can be bought for around 975 baht. Used mobile phones are even more reasonably priced.

PHOTOGRAPHY

Memory cards for digital cameras are less expensive than in the UK, as are prints of digital photos. Before photographing people, it's advisable to ask their permission – with a smile. This applies in particular if you wish to photograph Muslim Thais.

POST

Airmail to Europe up to 10 g costs 17 baht, postcards 15 baht. Delivery time is usually between five and seven days. Postage for parcels is determined according to weight and mode of transportation (by ship or airplane). Airmail packages with a weight of 10 kg cost 4,250 baht. Most post offices sell standard packages.

USEFUL PHRASES THAI

Letters in *italics* (masculine form) are to be replaced by the respective feminine form *[...]*, as necessary.

Yes/No	*krap [kah]* chai/mai chai	ครับ(ค่ะ) ใช่/ไม่ใช่
Please/Thank you	khaw ... noy/khop koon *krab [kah]*	ขอ...หน่อย/ขอบคุณครับ(ค่ะ)
Sorry	khaw toht	ขอโทษ !
Good afternoon!/evening!	sahwadee *krab [kah]*	สวัสดีครับ(ค่ะ)
Goodbye	sahwadee	สวัสดี !
My name is ...	chan joo ...	ฉันชื่อ ...
I'm from ...	chan ma jag ...	ฉันมาจาก ......
I don't understand you	chan mai khao jai koon	ฉันไม่เข้าใจคุณ
How much is ...?	nee laka taolai	นี่ราคาเท่าไร ?
Excuse me, where can I find ...?	khaw toht *krab [kah]* ... yuu tee nai	ขอโทษครับ(ค่ะ) ... อยู่ที่ไหน ?

1 nueng	หนึ่ง	5 hah	ห้า	9 gao	เก้า
2 song	สอง	6 hok	หก	10 sip	สิบ
3 sahm	สาม	7 jet	เจ็ด	20 yee sip	ยี่สิบ
4 see	สี่	8 beht	แปด	100 nueng loi	หนึ่งร้อย

PRICES & CURRENCY

The Thai baht (THB) is divided into 100 satang. Coins in 1, 2, 5 and 10 baht denominations and 20, 50, 100, 500 and 1,000 baht notes are in circulation. 25 and 50 satang coins are usually only found in supermarkets. In a modest restaurant a main course seldom more than 150 baht. In supermarkets you can buy a bottle of local beer for 30 to 50 baht. Thais do not consider it unfair to charge a "rich" foreigner higher prices. This not only applies to shopping at markets, but also hotels, zoos, museums, amusement parks etc. Even state-run institutions such as national parks operate on the two-tier pricing system.

PUBLIC TRANSPORT

The most important train routes run north from Bangkok, northeast up to the Laotian border and south to Malaysia and Singapore. Train timetables and fares: *www.railway.co.th.*
Direct buses take you from Bangkok to practically every large city in the country. The air-conditioned VIP buses with sleeper seats are quite comfortable (from Bangkok to Phuket approx. 980 baht).

TAXI

So-called *Meter Taxis,* which have their fare meter switched on, are only available in Bangkok and in Phuket at the airport. Everywhere else the price must be negotiated – preferably before you embark on your journey! The first kilometre in a *Meter Taxi* costs 35 baht, and every additional kilometre 5.50 Baht. For these prices it is almost impossible – at least for a tourist – to hire a three-wheel Tuk Tuk.

TIME

Thailand time is GMT plus 7 hours throughout the year (New York plus 14 hours, Australia minus 3 hours).

TIPPING & SERVICE CHARGES

Tipping is not commonplace in average restaurants or at food stands. The higher quality restaurants will add a service charge of 10 percent to your bill. Only leave a tip in these establishments if the service was outstanding. In restaurants that don't add the service charge, but have provided good service, a 10 percent tip is appropriate. Many hotels add a 10 percent service charge to the room rate. Bear in mind that porters and other service staff are grateful for a small gratuity. Tipping taxi drivers is not customary, especially if the price had to be negotiated.

TOURIST INFORMATION

THAILAND TOURIST AUTHORITY

UK: 17–19 Cockspur Street | London SW1Y 5BL | tel. 0870 900 2007 | www. tourismthailand.org

US: Broadway, Suite 2810 | New York, NY 10006 | tel. 212/432-0433 | www. tourismthailand.org

Australia: Level 20, 56 Pit Street | Sydney, NSW 2000 | tel. (02) 9247 7549 | www. tourismthailand.org

TOURISM AUTHORITY OF THAILAND (TAT)

The Tourism Authority of Thailand has offices in all major provincial capitals. Addresses for various offices are found in the chapters for the different regions, and e-mail addresses are listed on the website *www.tourismthailand.org.* You can find a wealth of information about Thailand on the Internet: *www.thaiwebsites.com, www.amazing-thailand.com, www.sawadee.com,* and *www.diningthailand.com* (restaurants). Weather information can be found at *www.tmd.go.th/en*

TOURIST POLICE

The *Tourist Police* is responsible for tourists, and can be reached by telephone nationwide: *Tel. 1155.*

VALUE ADDED TAX (VAT)

Many of the smarter stores, restaurants and hotels add a Value Added Tax (VAT) of 7 percent to the price. At other establishments it is simply *"VAT included"*. An increased VAT of 10 percent is panned, but has not been implemented so far. If you buy goods with a value of at least 5,000 baht (show your passport!) and spend a minimum of 2,000 baht per transaction, you can have the VAT reimbursed upon departure. Receipts must be presented to VAT offices at airports in Bangkok, Hat Yai, Chiang Mai and Phuket (the only locations where a refund is possible) prior to your departure. Among large crowds this can be a time-consuming process! It's no wonder a sign at the VAT counter in the Bangkok Airport warns: "Insulting officials will result in a penalty." Find out more at *www.rd.go.th/vrt*.

WEATHER IN BANGKOK

	Jan	Feb	March	April	May	June	July	Aug	Sept	Oct	Nov	Dec
Daytime temperatures in °C/°F	32/90	33/91	34/93	35/95	34/93	33/91	32/90	32/90	32/90	31/88	31/88	31/88
Nighttime temperatures in °C/°F	20/68	23/73	24/75	26/79	25/77	25/77	25/77	24/75	24/75	24/75	23/73	20/68
Sunshine hours/day	8	8	8	10	8	6	5	5	5	6	7	8
Precipitation days/month	1	2	3	4	13	14	15	15	17	13	4	1
Water temperature in °C/°F	26/79	27/81	27/81	28/82	28/82	28/82	28/82	28/82	28/82	27/81	27/81	27/81

Sunshine hours/day · Precipitation days/month · Water temperature in °C/°F

ROAD ATLAS

The green line indicates the Discovery Tour "Thailand at a glance"
The blue line indicates the other Discovery Tours

All tours are also marked on the pull-out map

Photo: Rice field at Chiang Mai

Exploring Thailand

The map on the back cover shows how the area has been sub-divided

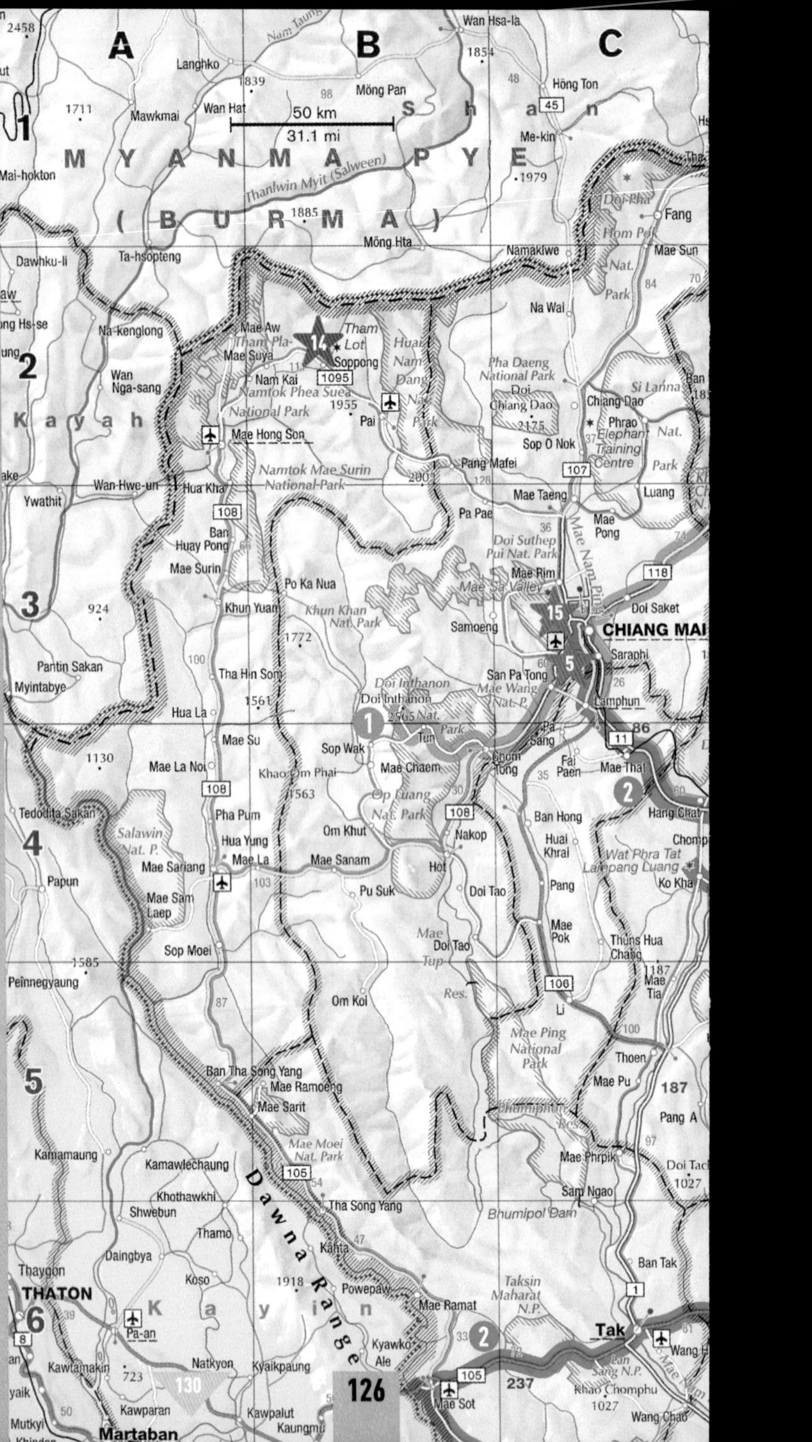
A
B
C
1
2
3
4
5
6
50 km
31.1 mi
MYANMA PYE
(BURMA)
Shan
Kayah
Kayin
Thanlwin Myit (Salween)
Dawna Range
Wan Hsa-la
Langhko
Möng Pan
Hong Ton
Mawkmai
Wan Hat
Me-kin
Mai-hokton
Möng Hta
Fang
Ta-hsopteng
Dawhku-li
Namakiwe
Mae Sun
Doi Pha Hom Pok Nat. Park
Na Wai
Na-kenglong
Mae Aw
Tham Pla
Tham Lot
Mae Suya
Soppong
Nam Kai
Huai Nam Dang Nat. Park
Pha Daeng National Park
Namtok Phea Suea National Park
Doi Chiang Dao
Chiang Dao
Si Lanna
Wan Nga-sang
Pai
Mae Hong Son
Sop O Nok
Phrao
Elephant Training Centre
Nat. Park
Namtok Mae Surin National Park
Pang Mafei
Wan-Hwe-un
Hua Kha
Ywathit
Mae Taeng
Luang
Pa Pae
Mae Pong
Ban Huay Pong
Doi Suthep Pui Nat. Park
Mae Surin
Mae Rim
Po Ka Nua
Mae Sa Valley
Mae Nam Ping
Doi Saket
Khun Yuam
Khun Khan Nat. Park
Samoeng
CHIANG MAI
Saraphi
Pantin Sakan
Tha Hin Som
San Pa Tong
Myintabye
Doi Inthanon
Mae Wang Nat. P.
Hua La
Doi Inthanon Nat. Park
Lamphun
Mae Su
Sop Wak
Tun
Pa Sang
Chom Tong
Mae La Noi
Mae Chaem
Fai Paen
Mae That
Khao Om Phai
Op Luang Nat. Park
Tedodita Sakan
Pha Pum
Ban Hong
Hang Chat
Salawin Nat. P.
Hua Yung
Om Khut
Nakop
Huai Khrai
Wat Phra Tat Lampang Luang
Mae Sariang
Mae La
Mae Sanam
Hot
Papun
Pu Suk
Doi Tao
Pang
Ko Kha
Mae Sam Laep
Mae Pok
Mae Doi Tao Tup Res.
Thuns Hua Chang
Sop Moei
Peinnegyaung
Om Koi
Mae Tia
Li
Mae Ping National Park
Thoen
Ban Tha Song Yang
Mae Ramoeng
Mae Pu
Mae Sarit
Bhumiphon Res.
Pang A
Kamamaung
Mae Moei Nat. Park
Kamawlechaung
Mae Phrpik
Doi Tac
Khothawkhi
Tha Song Yang
Sam Ngao
Shwebun
Bhumipol Dam
Thamo
Kahta
Daingbya
Ban Tak
Thaygon
Koso
Powepaw
Taksin Maharat N.P.
THATON
Mae Ramat
Tak
Pa-an
Kyawko
Ale
Lan Sang N.P.
Natkyon
Kyaikpaung
Kawtamakin
Mae Sot
Khao Chomphu
Kawparan
Kawpalut
Kaungmu
Wang Chao
Mutkyi
Martaban
126
130
45
107
108
118
11
1095
106
105
1
8
14
15
5
2

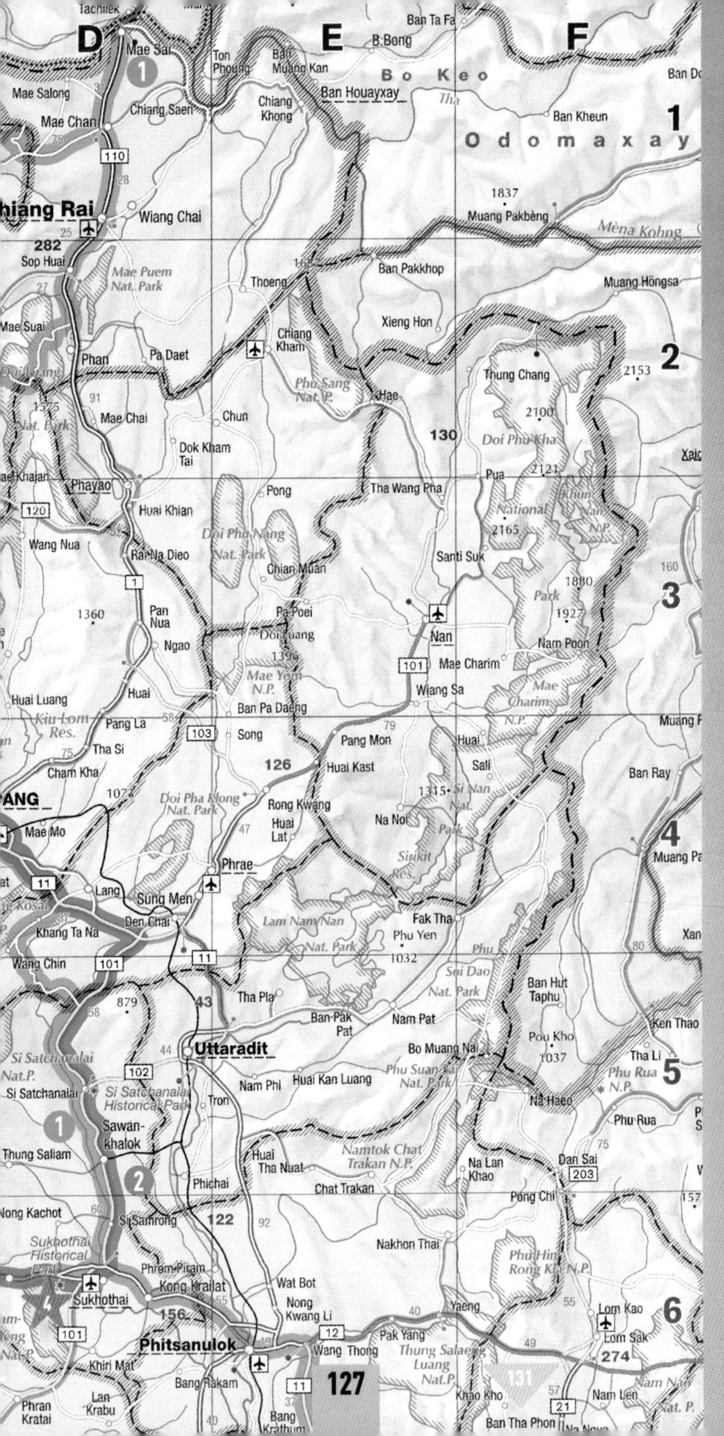

D
E
F
1
2
3
4
5
6
Mae Sai
Chiang Saen
Mae Chan
Mae Salong
Chiang Rai
Wiang Chai
Ton Phoung
Ban Muang Kan
Chiang Khong
Ban Houayxay
Bo Keo
Ban Ta Fa
B.Bong
Ban Kheun
Odomaxay
Muang Pakbèng
Mèna Kohng
Ban Pakkhop
Muang Hôngsa
Xieng Hon
Thoeng
Chiang Kham
Sop Huai
Mae Puem Nat. Park
Mae Suai
Phan
Pa Daet
Phu Sang Nat. P.
Hae
Thung Chang
Doi Phu Kha
Mae Chai
Chun
Dok Kham Tai
Phayao
Huai Khian
Pong
Tha Wang Pha
Pua
Khun Nan N.P.
National Park
Wang Nua
Doi Phu Nang Nat. Park
Chian Muan
Santi Suk
Pan Nua
Ngao
Pa Poei
Doi Luang
Nan
Mae Charim
Nam Poon
Mae Yom N.P.
Wiang Sa
Mae Charim N.P.
Huai Luang
Huai
Ban Pa Daeng
Kiu Lom Res.
Pang La
Tha Si
Song
Pang Mon
Huai Kast
Sali
Cham Kha
Doi Pha Klong Nat. Park
Rong Kwang
Huai Lat
Na Noi
Si Nan Nat. Park
Ban Ray
Mae Mo
Phrae
Sirikit Res.
Muang Pa
Lang
Sung Men
Den Chai
Khang Ta Na
Lam Nam Nan Nat. Park
Fak Tha
Phu Yen
Wang Chin
Phu Soi Dao Nat. Park
Ban Hut Taphu
Tha Pla
Ban Pak Pat
Nam Pat
Ken Thao
Uttaradit
Bo Muang Nai
Pou Kho
Tha Li
Si Satchanalai Nat.P.
Si Satchanalai
Si Satchanalai Historical Park
Nam Phi
Huai Kan Luang
Phu Suan Sai Nat. Park
Tron
Na Haeo
Phu Rua N.P.
Phu Rua
Sawan-khalok
Thung Saliam
Huai Tha Nuat
Namtok Chat Trakan N.P.
Na Lan Khao
Dan Sai
Phichai
Chat Trakan
Pong Chi
Si Samrong
Nakhon Thai
Sukhothai Historical Park
Phu Hin Rong Kla N.P.
Phrom Piram
Wat Bot
Sukhothai
Kong Krailat
Nong Kwang Li
Yaeng
Lom Kao
Lom Sak
Phitsanulok
Pak Yang
Wang Thong
Thung Salaeng Luang Nat.P.
Khiri Mat
Bang Rakam
Nam Nao Nat. P.
Phran Kratai
Lan Krabu
Bang Krathum
Khao Kho
Nam Len
Ban Tha Phon
110
1
120
103
101
11
102
12
203
21
274
131

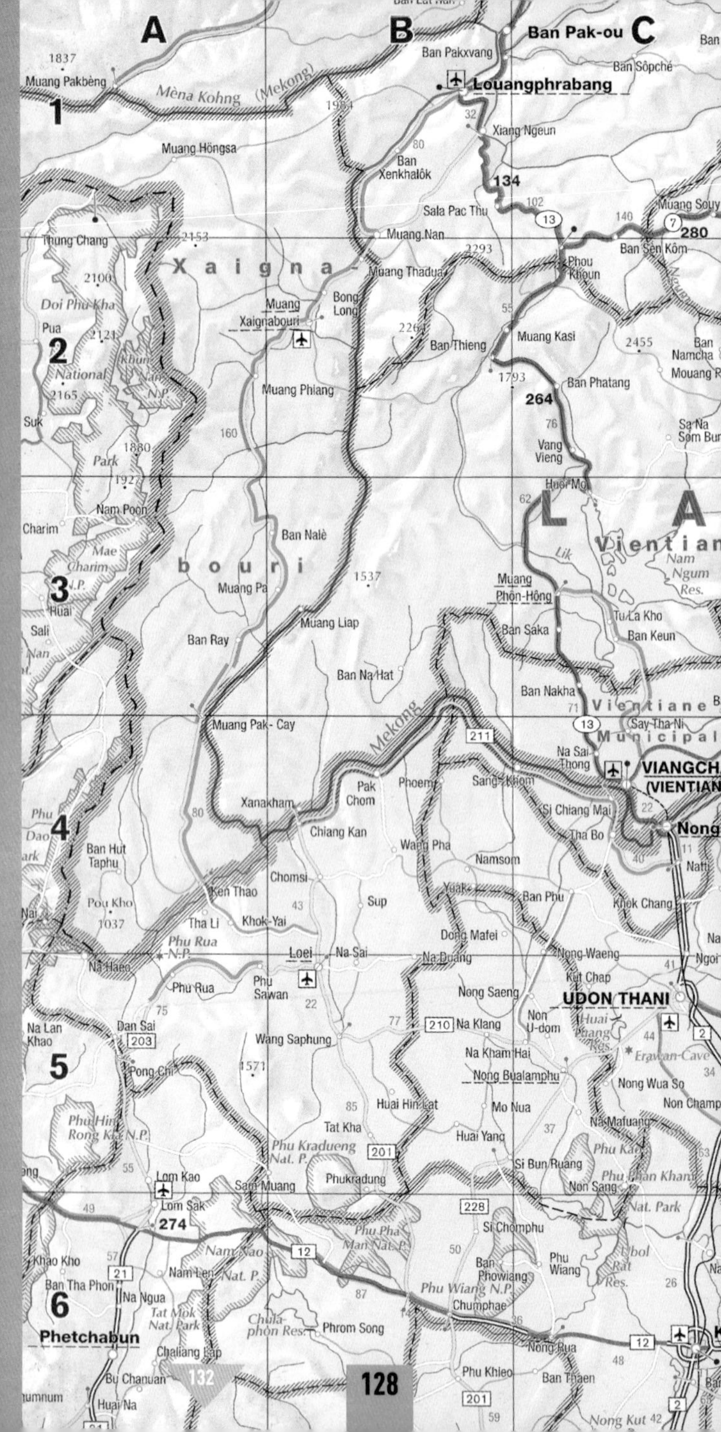

A
B
C
1
2
3
4
5
6
Ban Pak-ou
Ban Pakxvang
Ban Sôpchè
Louangphrabang
Muang Pakbèng
Mèna Kohng (Mekong)
Xiang Ngeun
Muang Höngsa
Ban Xenkhalôk
Sala Pac Thu
Muang Souy
Thung Chang
Muang Nan
Ban Sen Kôm
Phou Khoun
Muang Thadua
Xaignabouri
Muang Xaignabouri
Bong Long
Doi Phu Kha
Ban Thieng
Muang Kasi
Ban Namcha
Pua
Khun Nan National Park
Ban Phatang
Muang Phiang
Suk
Vang Vieng
Sa Na Som Bun
Huei Mo
Charim
Nam Poon
Ban Nalè
LA
Vientian
Mae Charim N.P.
Nam Ngum Res.
Lik
Muang Pa
Muang Phôn-Hông
Huai
Sali
Nan
Muang Liap
Tu La Kho
Ban Ray
Ban Saka
Ban Keun
Ban Na Hat
Ban Nakha
Vientiane Municipal
Muang Pak-Cay
Mekong
Say Tha Ni
Na Sai Thong
VIANGCHA
(VIENTIAN
Pak Chom
Phoem
Sang Khom
Phu Dao
Xanakham
Si Chiang Mai
Chiang Kan
Tha Bo
Nong
Ban Hut Taphu
Wang Pha
Natt
Namsom
Chomsi
Ken Thao
Sup
Ban Phu
Khok Chang
Pou Kho
Tha Li
Khok-Yai
Dong Mafei
Phu Rua N.P.
Loei
Na Sai
Na Duang
Nong Waeng
Na Haeo
Phu Rua
Phu Sawan
Kut Chap
Nong Saeng
UDON THANI
Na Lan Khao
Dan Sai
Wang Saphung
Non U-dom
Na Klang
Huai Luang Res.
Na Kham Hai
Erawan Cave
Pong Chi
Nong Bualamphu
Nong Wua So
Phu Hin Rong Kla N.P.
Huai Hin Lat
Mo Nua
Non Champa
Tat Kha
Na Mafuang
Huai Yang
Phu Kradueng Nat. P.
Phu Kao
Si Bun Ruang
Phu Phan Kham
Lom Kao
Sam Muang
Phukradung
Non Sang
Lom Sak
Nat. Park
Si Chomphu
Phu Pha Man Nat. P.
Nam Nao Nat. P.
Ubol Rat Res.
Khao Kho
Nam Len
Ban Phowiang
Phu Wiang
Ban Tha Phon
Na Ngua
Phu Wiang N.P.
Chumphae
Tat Mok Nat. Park
Chulaphon Res.
Phrom Song
Phetchabun
Chaliang Lap
Nong Rua
Bu Chanuan
Phu Khieo
Ban Thaen
Huai Na
Nong Kut

132

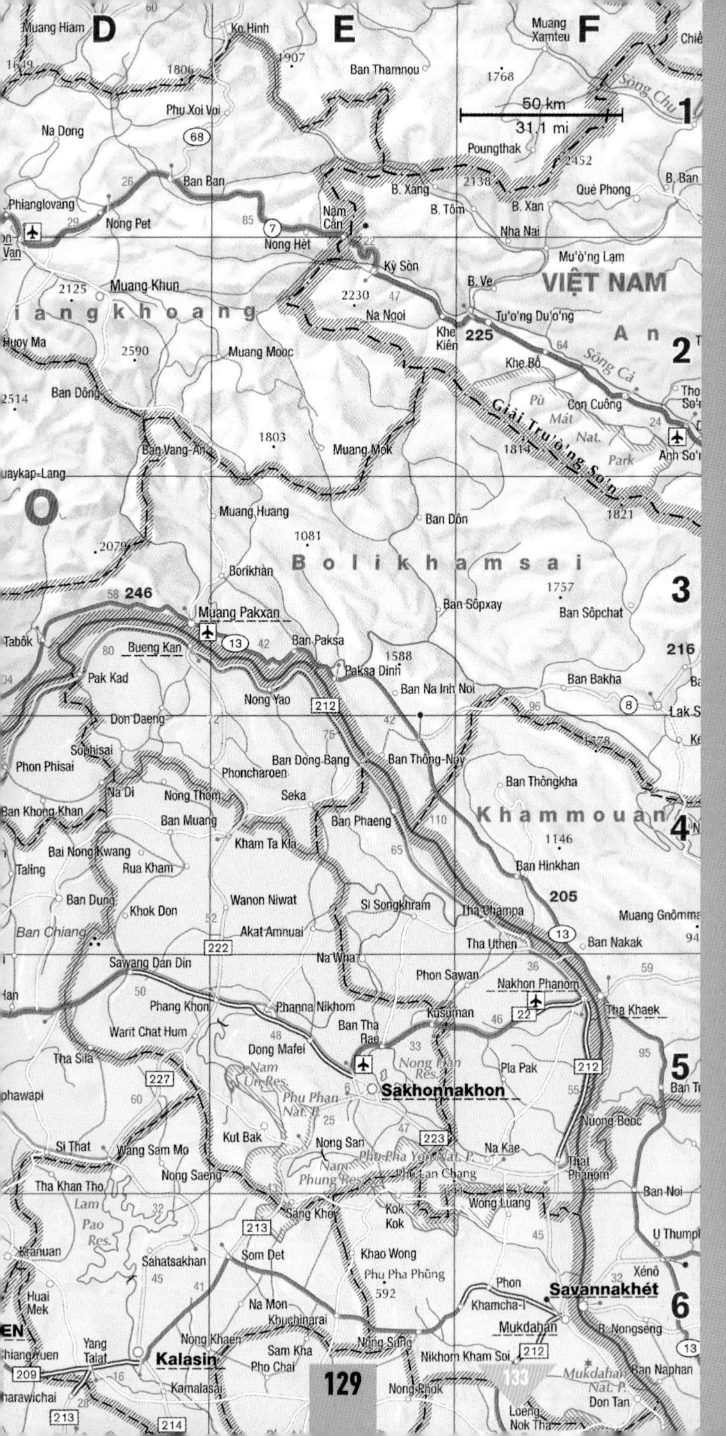
D
E
F
1
2
3
4
5
6
Muang Hiam
Ko Hinh
1907
Ban Thamnou
Muang Xamteu
1768
Song Chu
1806
Phu Xoi Voi
50 km
31,1 mi
Na Dong
68
Poungthak
2452
26
Ban Ban
B. Xang
2138
Qué Phong
B. Ban
Phianglovang
29
Nong Pet
85
7
Nậm Cắn
B. Tôm
B. Xan
Nha Nai
Nong Hèt
22
Kỳ Sòn
Mư'ò'ng Lạm
2125
Muang Khun
2230
47
B. Ve
VIỆT NAM
iangkhoang
Na Ngoi
Khe Kiên
225
Tư'ơ'ng Dư'ơ'ng
An
Huoy Ma
2590
Muang Mooc
64
Sông Cả
Khe Bố
2514
Ban Dông
Pù Mát Nat. Park
Con Cuông
Giải Trư'ờ'ng Sơ'n
24
Anh So'
1803
Ban Vang-An
Muang Mok
1814
uaykap-Lang
1821
O
Muang Huang
Ban Dôn
1081
2079
Borikhàn
Bolikhamsai
1757
3
58
246
Muang Pakxan
Ban Sôpxay
Ban Sôpchat
Tabôk
13
42
Ban Paksa
216
80
Bueng Kan
1588
Pak Kad
Paksa Dinh
Ban Na Inh Noi
Ban Bakha
Nong Yao
212
96
8
Lak S
Don Daeng
72
42
75
1378
Sophisai
Phon Phisai
Ban Dong Bang
Ban Thông-Noy
Ban Thôngkha
Phoncharoen
Na Di
Nong Thom
Seka
Ban Khong Khan
Ban Muang
Ban Phaeng
110
Khammouan
Kham Ta Kla
1146
Bai Nong Kwang
65
Taling
Rua Kham
Ban Hinkhan
Ban Dung
Wanon Niwat
205
Khok Don
Si Songkhram
Tha Champa
Muang Gnômma
Ban Chiang
52
Akat Amnuai
13
222
Tha Uthen
Ban Nakak
Sawang Dan Din
Na Wha
36
59
Phon Sawan
50
Nakhon Phanom
Phang Khon
Phanna Nikhom
Kusuman
22
Tha Khaek
Warit Chat Hum
46
Ban Tha Rae
48
33
Dong Mafei
Nong Han Res.
95
Tha Sila
Nam Un Res.
Pla Pak
212
227
Sakhonnakhon
Ban Tı
Phu Phan Nat. P.
55
60
25
Nuong Booc
Si That
Wang Sam Mo
Kut Bak
Nong San
223
Na Kae
That Phanom
Phu Pha Yon Nat. P.
Nong Saeng
Nam Phung Res.
Phu Lan Chang
Tha Khan Tho
Ban Noi
Lam Pao Res.
43
32
Sang Kho
Wong Luang
Kok Kok
213
45
U Thump
Kranuan
Sahatsakhan
Som Det
Khao Wong
45
Phu Pha Phũng
Xénô
32
Phon
Savannakhét
Huai Mek
41
592
Na Mon
Khamcha-I
Kuchinarai
B. Nongseng
Mukdahan
Nong Khaen
Nong Sung
Yang Talat
Sam Kha
13
Kalasin
Nikhom Kham Soi
212
Phao Chai
209
16
Mukdahan Nat. P.
Ban Naphan
Kamalasai
Nong Phok
Don Tan
harawichai
28
133
Loeng Nok Tha
213
214

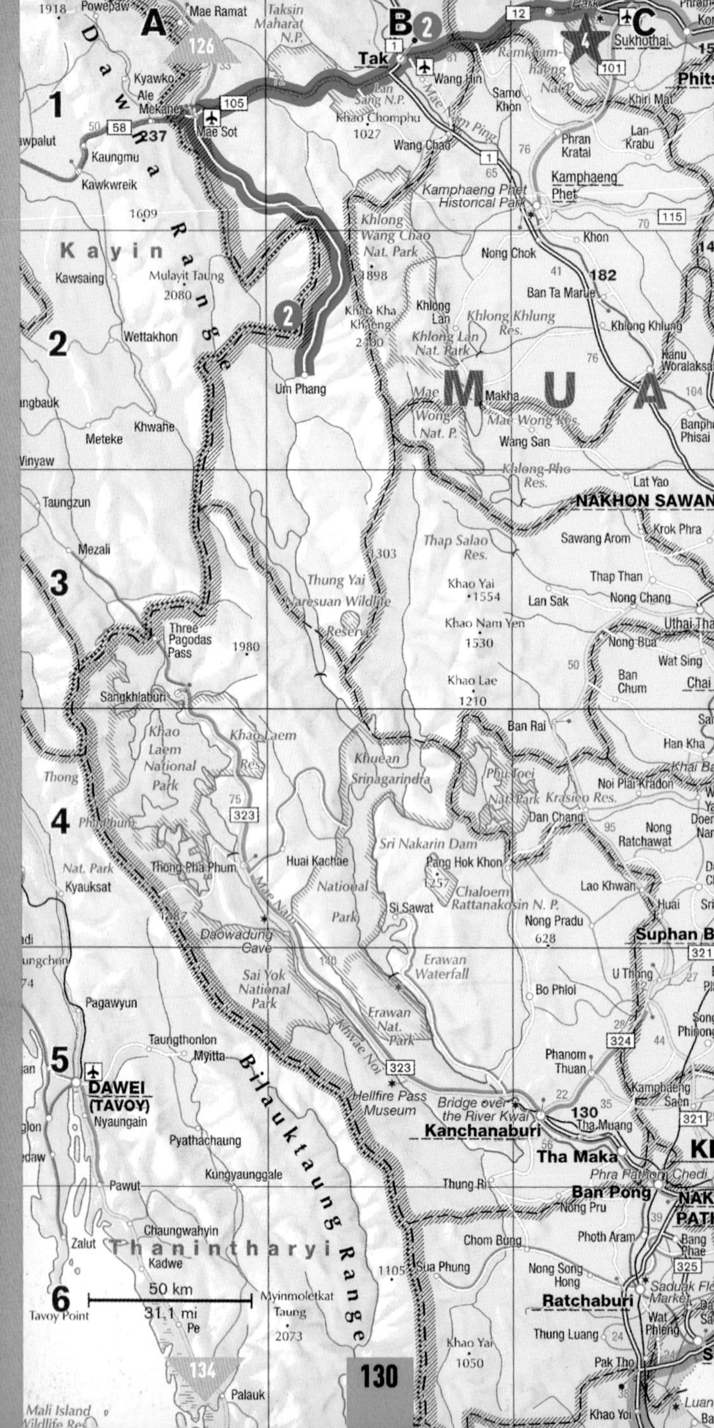

A
B
C
Mae Ramat
Taksin Maharat N.P.
Tak
Wang Hin
Sukhothai
Ramkhamhaeng Nat. P.
Dawna Range
Kyawko
Mekane
Mae Sot
Lan Sang N.P.
Khao Chomphu
1027
Samo Khon
Kiri Mat
Wang Chao
Mae Nam Ping
Phran Kratai
Lan Krabu
Kaungmu
Kawkwreik
Kamphaeng Phet Historical Park
Kamphaeng Phet
Khlong Wang Chao Nat. Park
Kayin
Mulayit Taung
2080
Kawsaing
Nong Chok
Khon
Ban Ta Marue
Khlong Khlung
Khao Kha Khaeng
Khlong Lan
Khlong Khlung Res.
Khlong Lan Nat. Park
Wettakhon
Um Phang
M U A
Mae Wong Nat. P.
Makha
Mae Wong Res.
Wang San
Meteke
Khwahe
Khlong Pho Res.
Lat Yao
NAKHON SAWAN
Taungzun
Mezali
Thap Salao Res.
Sawang Arom
Krok Phra
Thap Than
Thung Yai Naresuan Wildlife Reserve
Khao Yai
1554
Lan Sak
Nong Chang
Three Pagodas Pass
Khao Nam Yen
1530
Nong Bua
Wat Sing
Ban Chum
Khao Lae
1210
Sangkhlaburi
Khao Laem National Park
Khao Laem Res.
Ban Rai
Han Kha
Khuean Srinagarindra
Phu Toei Nat. Park
Krasieo Res.
Noi Plai Kradon
Dan Chang
Nong Ratchawat
Sri Nakarin Dam
Thong Pha Phum
Huai Kachae National Park
Pang Hok Khon
1257
Chaloem Rattanakosin N. P.
Kyauksat
Si Sawat
Nong Pradu
628
Lao Khwan
Daowadung Cave
Erawan Waterfall
Suphan Buri
Sai Yok National Park
U Thong
Bo Phloi
Pagawyun
Erawan Nat. Park
Song Phi Nong
Taungthonlon
Myitta
Phanom Thuan
Bilauktaung Range
DAWEI (TAVOY)
Nyaungain
Hellfire Pass Museum
Bridge over the River Kwai
Kanchanaburi
Tha Muang
Kamphaeng Saen
Pyathachaung
Tha Maka
Kungyaunggale
Phra Pathom Chedi
Pawut
Thung Ri
Ban Pong
Nong Pru
Chaungwahyin
Chom Bung
Photh Aram
Bang Phae
Zalut
Thanintharyi
Kadwe
Sua Phung
Nong Song Hong
Saduak Floating Market
50 km
31.1 mi
Tavoy Point
Myinmoletkat Taung
2073
Ratchaburi
Wat Phleng
Thung Luang
Khao Yai
1050
Pak Tho
Palauk
Khao Yoi
Mali Island Wildlife Res.

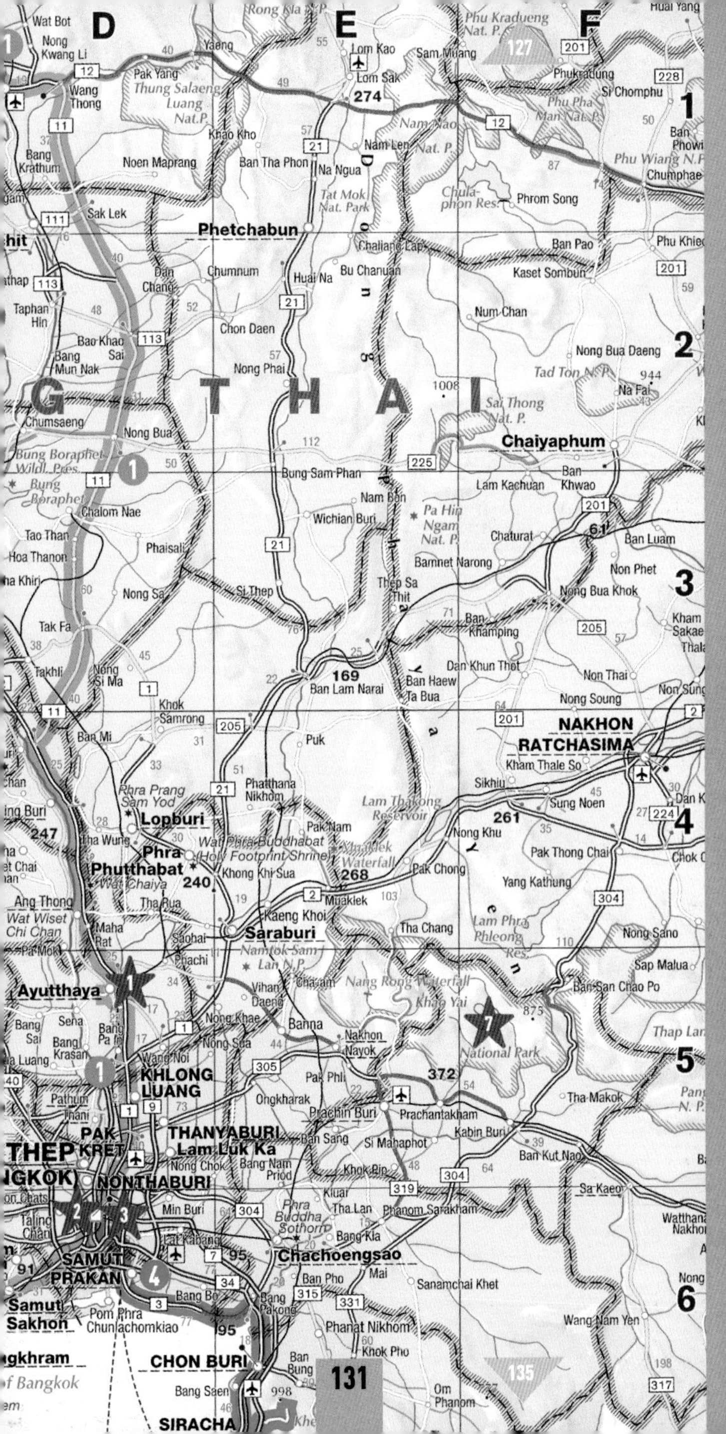

D
E
F
1
2
3
4
5
6
THAI
127
135
131
Wat Bot
Nong Kwang Li
Wang Thong
Pak Yang
Thung Salaeng Luang Nat.P.
Yaeng
Rong Kla N.P.
Lom Kao
Lom Sak
Sam Muang
Phu Kradueng Nat. P.
Phukradung
Si Chomphu
Phu Pha Man Nat. P.
Nam Nao Nat. P.
Phu Wiang N.P.
Chumphae
Khao Kho
Bang Krathum
Noen Maprang
Ban Tha Phon
Nam Len
Na Ngua
Tat Mok Nat. Park
Chulaphon Res.
Phrom Song
Sak Lek
Phetchabun
Chaliang Lap
Ban Pao
Phu Khiao
Kaset Sombun
Dan Chang
Chumnum
Huai Na
Bu Chanuan
Taphan Hin
Bao Khao Sai
Bang Mun Nak
Chon Daen
Num Chan
Nong Bua Daeng
Tad Ton N.P.
Na Fai
Nong Phai
Sai Thong Nat. P.
Chumsaeng
Nong Bua
Chaiyaphum
Bung Boraphet Wildl. Pres.
Bung Boraphet
Bung Sam Phan
Lam Kachuan
Ban Khwao
Chalom Nae
Nam Bon
Wichian Buri
Pa Hin Ngam Nat. P.
Chaturat
Ban Luam
Tao Than
Hoa Thanon
Phaisali
Bamnet Narong
Non Phet
Nong Sa
Si Thep
Thep Sa Thit
Nong Bua Khok
Tak Fa
Ban Khamping
Kham Sakae
Takhli
Nong Si Ma
Ban Lam Narai
Ban Haew Ta Bua
Dan Khun Thot
Non Thai
Nong Soung
Khok Samrong
Ban Mi
Puk
NAKHON RATCHASIMA
Kham Thale So
Phra Prang Sam Yod
Phatthana Nikhom
Sikhiu
Lam Thakong Reservoir
Sung Noen
Lopburi
Pak Nam
Nong Khu
Tha Wung
Wat Phra Buddhabat (Holy Footprint Shrine)
Muak Lek Waterfall
Pak Thong Chai
Phra Phutthabat
Wat Chaiya
Khong Khi Sua
Pak Chong
Yang Kathung
Ang Thong
Tha Rua
Muaklek
Wat Wiset Chi Chan
Kaeng Khoi
Saraburi
Tha Chang
Lam Phra Phleong Res.
Nong Sano
Maha Rat
Saohai
Namtok Sam Lan N.P.
Sap Malua
Pa Mok
Phachi
Cha-am
Nang Rong Waterfall
Khao Yai National Park
Ban San Chao Po
Ayutthaya
Vihan Daeng
Bang Sai
Sena
Bang Pa In
Nong Khae
Banna
Bang Krasan
Nong Sua
Nakhon Nayok
Wang Noi
KHLONG LUANG
Pak Phli
Pathum Thani
Ongkharak
Prachin Buri
Prachantakham
Tha Makok
PAK KRET
THANYABURI
Lam Luk Ka
Ban Sang
Si Mahaphot
Kabin Buri
Ban Kut Nao
Nong Chok
Bang Nam Priod
Khok Pip
NONTHABURI
Sa Kaeo
Min Buri
Kluar
Phra Buddha Sothorn
Tha Lan
Phanom Sarakham
Taling Chan
Bang Kla
Lat Krabang
Chachoengsao
SAMUT PRAKAN
Mai
Ban Pho
Sanamchai Khet
Bang Bo
Bang Pakong
Samut Sakhon
Pom Phra Chunlachomkiao
Phanat Nikhom
Wang Nam Yen
Khok Pho
CHON BURI
Ban Bung
Bang Saen
Om Phanom
SIRACHA

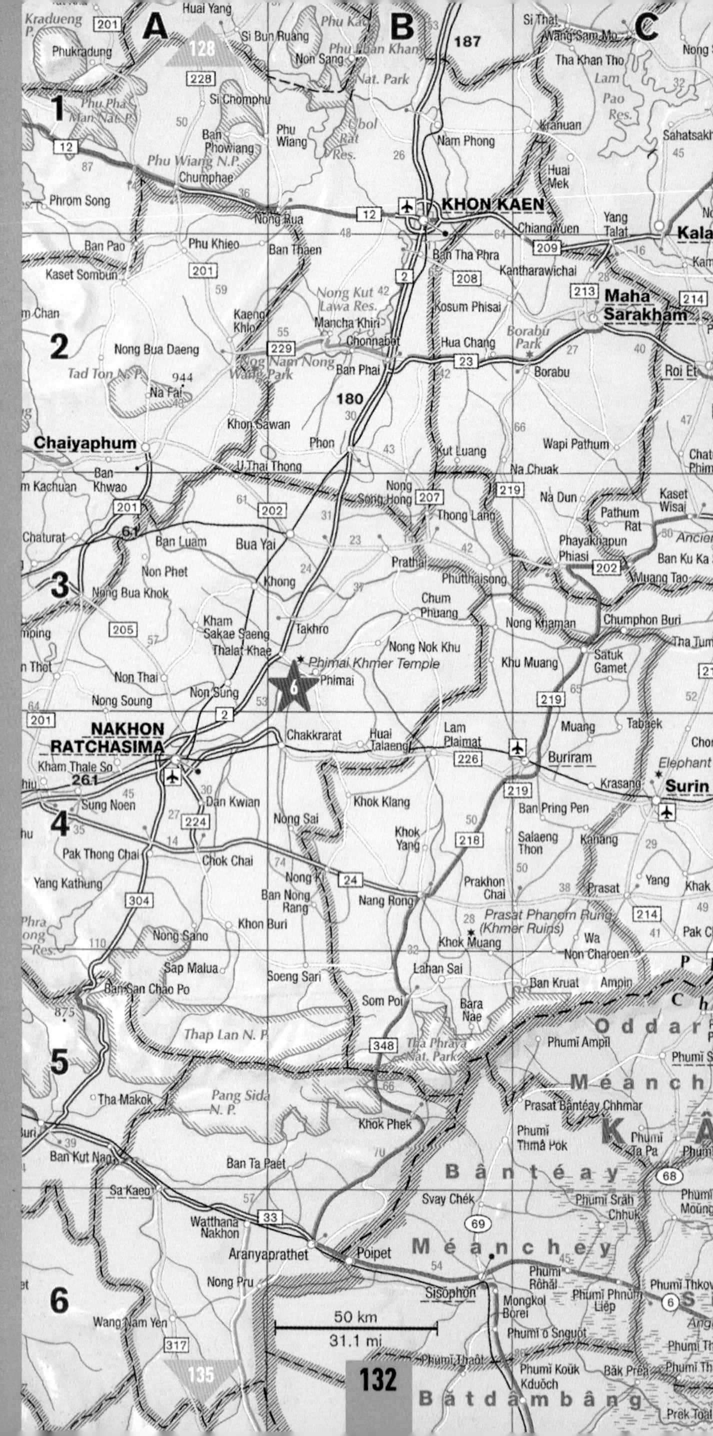

A
B
C
1
2
3
4
5
6
KHON KAEN
Chaiyaphum
NAKHON RATCHASIMA
Maha Sarakham
Buriram
Surin
Roi Et
Phimai Khmer Temple
Phimai
Prasat Phanom Rung (Khmer Ruins)
Thap Lan N. P.
Pang Sida N. P.
Aranyaprathet
Poipet
Sisophon
Oddar Méanchey
Bântéay Méanchey
Bătdâmbâng
50 km
31.1 mi

128
135

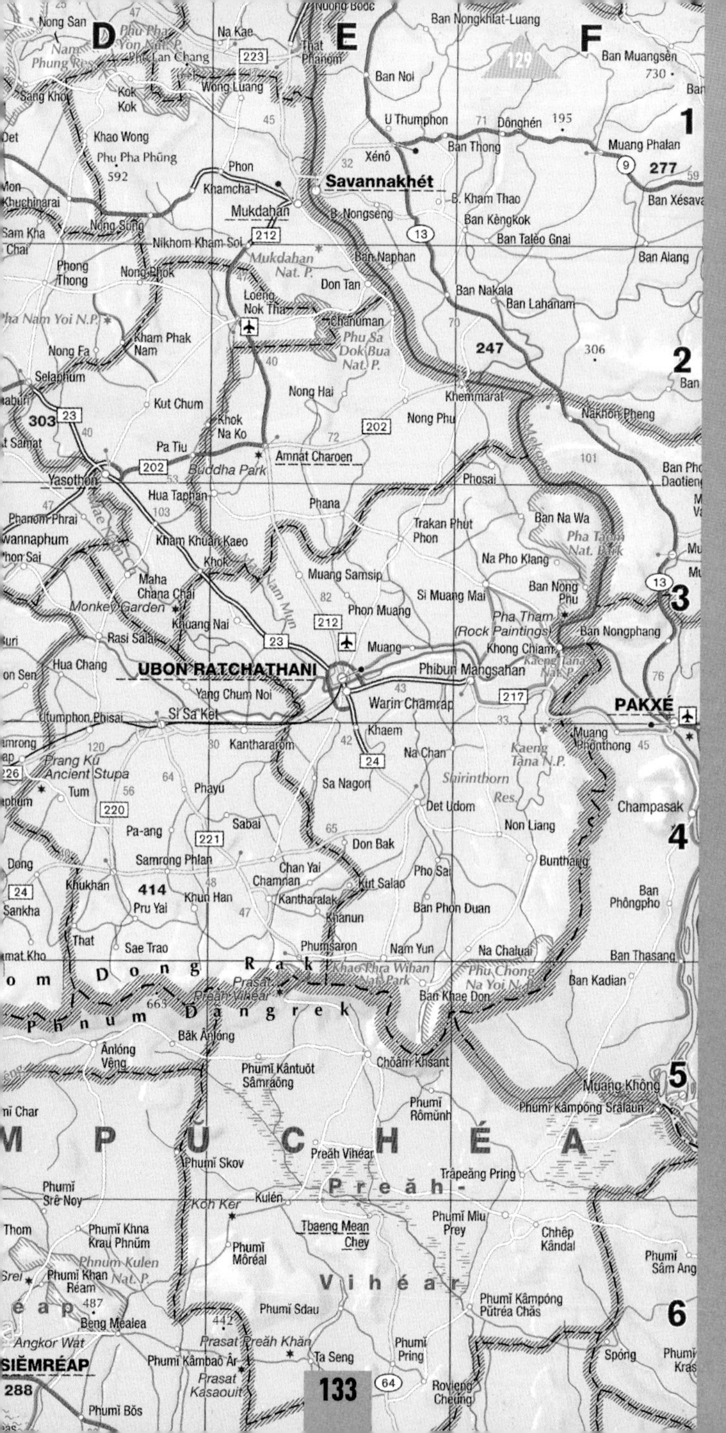
D
E
F
1
2
3
4
5
6
129
Nong San
Phu Pha Yon Nat. P.
Nam Phung Res.
Phu Lan Chang
Na Kae
223
That Phanom
Ban Nongkhiat-Luang
Ban Muangsen
730
Sang Khom
Kok Kok
Wong Luang
Ban Noi
Khao Wong
U Thumphon
71
Dônghén
195
Phu Pha Phũng
592
Phon
Xénô
Ban Thong
Muang Phalan
9
277
Khamcha-I
Savannakhét
Mukdahan
B. Kham Thao
Ban Xésava
Khuchinarai
B. Nongseng
Ban Kèngkok
Sam Kha Chai
Nong Sung
Nikhom Kham Soi
212
13
Ban Taléo Gnai
Ban Alang
Mukdahan Nat. P.
Ban Naphan
Phong Thong
Nong Phok
Don Tan
Loeng Nok Tha
Ban Nakala
Ban Lahanam
Chanuman
Phu Sa Dok Bua Nat. P.
247
306
Nong Fa
Kham Phak Nam
Selaphum
Nong Hai
Khemmarat
Kut Chum
Nakhon Pheng
303
23
Khok Na Ko
202
Nong Phu
Pa Tiu
Amnat Charoen
Buddha Park
101
Mekong
Yasothon
Hua Taphan
Phosai
Ban Pho Daotieng
Phana
Phanom Phrai
Trakan Phut Phon
Ban Na Wa
Pha Taem Nat. Park
Kham Khuan Kaeo
Khok
Na Pho Klang
Muang Samsip
Maha Chana Chai
Si Muang Mai
Ban Nong Phu
Monkey Garden
Phon Muang
Pha Tham (Rock Paintings)
Khuang Nai
Rasi Salai
Muang
Ban Nongphang
Khong Chiam
Hua Chang
UBON RATCHATHANI
Phibun Mangsahan
Kaeng Tana Nat. P.
Yang Chum Noi
Warin Chamrap
217
PAKXÉ
Si Sa Ket
Uthumphon Phisai
Kanthararom
Khaem
Muang Phonthong
Prang Ku Ancient Stupa
Na Chan
Kaeng Tana N.P.
Tum
Phayu
Sa Nagon
Sirinthorn Res.
220
Det Udom
Champasak
Pa-ang
Sabai
221
Don Bak
Non Liang
Samrong Phlan
Chan Yai
Chamnan
Pho Sai
Buntharig
Khukhan
414
Kut Salao
Pru Yai
Khun Han
Kantharalak
Ban Phon Duan
Ban Phôngpho
Sankha
Khanun
That
Sae Trao
Phumsaron
Nam Yun
Na Chaluai
Ban Thasang
Khao Phra Wihan Nat. Park
Phu Chong Na Yoi N.P.
Ban Kadian
D o n g R a k
Prasat Preăh Vihéar
Ban Khae Don
665
P h n u m D â n g r e k
Băk Ânlóng
Ânlóng Vêng
Phumĭ Kântuŏt Sâmraông
Chŏam Khsant
Muang Không
Phumĭ Rômúnh
Phumĭ Kâmpong Sralaun
M P U C H É A
Phumĭ Skov
Preăh Vihéar
Trâpeăng Pring
Phumĭ Srê Noy
Koh Ker
Kulén
P r e ă h -
Phumĭ Mlu Prey
Thom
Phumĭ Khna Krau Phnŭm
Tbaeng Mean Chey
Chhêp Kândal
Phumĭ Môréal
Phnum Kulen Nat. P.
Phumĭ Khan Réam
Phumĭ Sâm Ang
V i h é a r
487
Phumĭ Kâmpóng Pŭtréa Chăs
Beng Mealea
Phumĭ Sdau
442
Angkor Wat
Prasat Preăh Khăn
Ta Seng
Phumĭ Pring
Spóng
SIĔMRÉAP
Phumĭ Kâmbaô Âr
Prasat Kasaouit
64
Rovieng Cheung
288
Phumĭ Bŏs

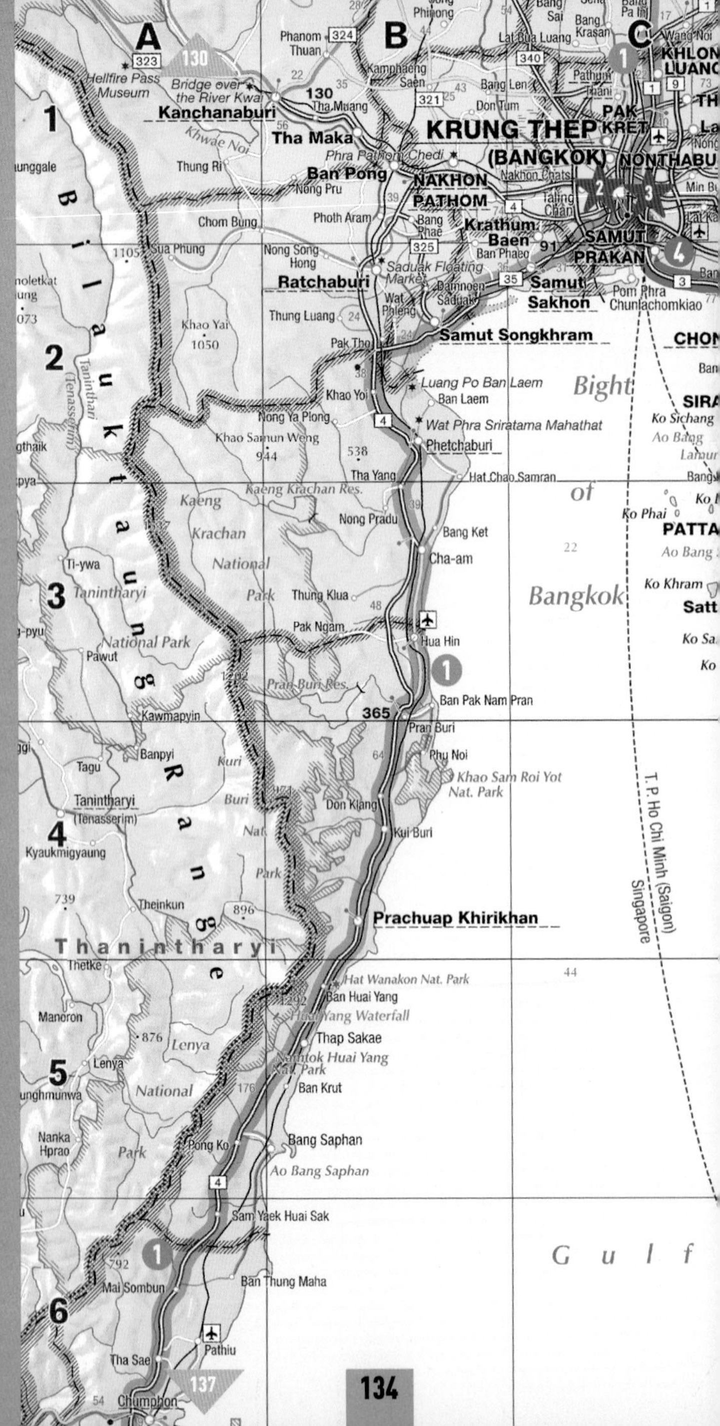

A
B
C
Kanchanaburi
Bridge over the River Kwai
Hellfire Pass Museum
Tha Maka
KRUNG THEP (BANGKOK)
NAKHON PATHOM
Ban Pong
Ratchaburi
Saduak Floating Market
Samut Sakhon
Samut Songkhram
SAMUT PRAKAN
Krathum Baen
Phetchaburi
Luang Po Ban Laem
Wat Phra Sriratama Mahathat
Kaeng Krachan Res.
Kaeng Krachan National Park
Cha-am
Hua Hin
Pran Buri Res.
Pran Buri
Khao Sam Roi Yot Nat. Park
Kui Buri
Kuri Buri Nat. Park
Prachuap Khirikhan
Hat Wanakon Nat. Park
Huai Yang Waterfall
Namtok Huai Yang Nat. Park
Thap Sakae
Ban Krut
Bang Saphan
Ao Bang Saphan
Sam Yaek Huai Sak
Ban Thung Maha
Pathiu
Tha Sae
Chumphon
Bilauktaung Range
Thanintharyi
Tanintharyi National Park
Lenya National Park
Tanintharyi (Tenasserim)
Bight of Bangkok
Gulf
T.P. Ho Chi Minh (Saigon) Singapore
Ko Sichang
Ko Phai
Ko Khram
Pom Phra Chunlachomkiao

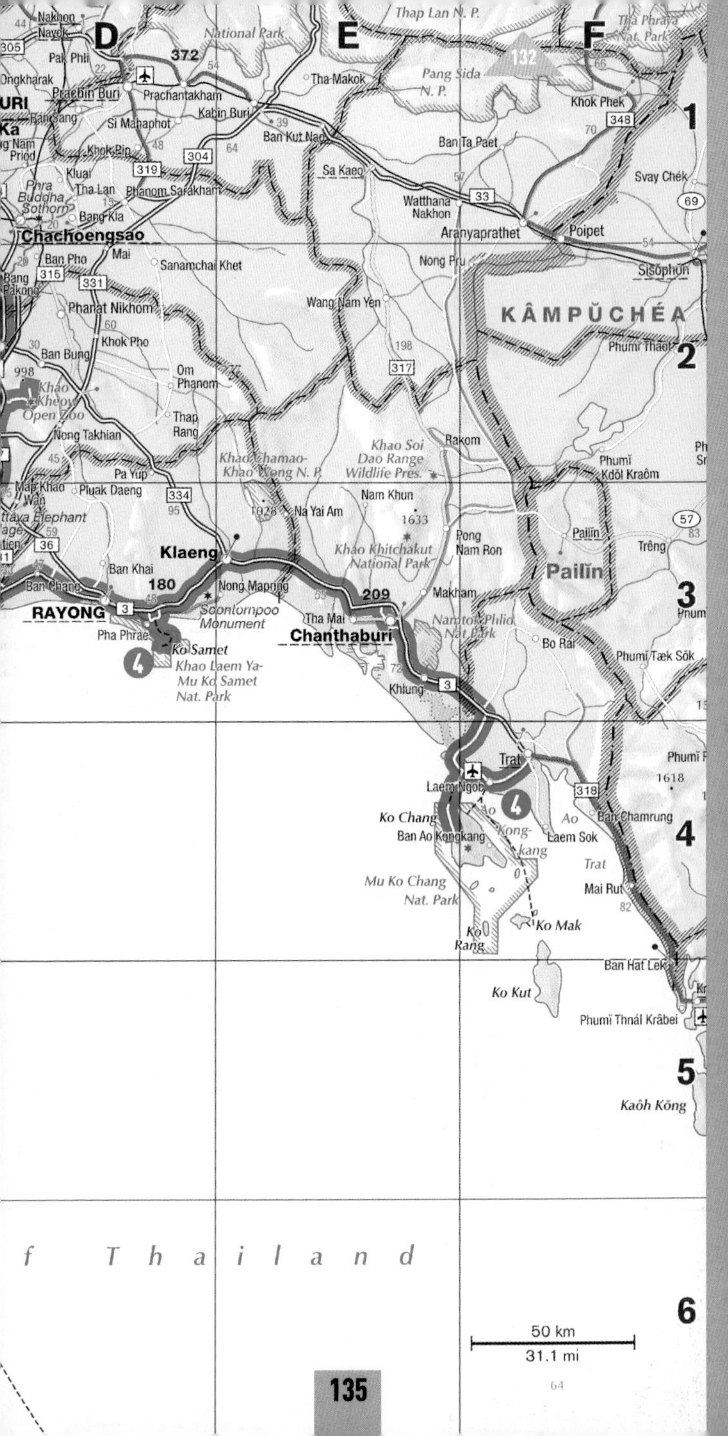
D
E
F
1
2
3
4
5
6
Prachin Buri
Prachantakham
Kabin Buri
Tha Makok
Pang Sida N. P.
Thap Lan N. P.
Tha Phraya Nat. Park
Khok Phek
Ban Kut Nao
Ban Ta Paet
Svay Chék
Sa Kaeo
Watthana Nakhon
Aranyaprathet
Poipet
Nong Pru
Sisŏphŏn
Chachoengsao
Phanom Sarakham
Si Mahaphot
Khok Pip
Tha Lan
Bang Kla
Phra Buddha Sothorn
Ban Pho
Mai
Sanamchai Khet
Phanat Nikhom
Khok Pho
Ban Bung
Wang Nam Yen
KÂMPŬCHÉA
Phumĭ Thaot
Om Phanom
Thap Rang
Khao Kheow Open Zoo
Nong Takhian
Khao Chamao-Khao Wong N. P.
Khao Soi Dao Range Wildlife Pres.
Rakom
Phumĭ Kdŏl Kraôm
Pa Yup
Pluak Daeng
Nam Khun
Na Yai Am
Khao Khitchakut National Park
Pong Nam Ron
Pailĭn
Trêng
Klaeng
Ban Khai
Ban Chang
RAYONG
Nong Mapring
Soonlornpoo Monument
Makham
Tha Mai
Chanthaburi
Namtok Phlio Nat. Park
Bo Rai
Phumĭ Tæk Sŏk
Pha Phrae
Ko Samet
Khao Laem Ya-Mu Ko Samet Nat. Park
Khlung
Trat
Laem Ngob
Ko Chang
Ban Ao Kongkang
Ao Kong-kang
Ao Trat
Laem Sok
Ban Chamrung
Mu Ko Chang Nat. Park
Mai Rut
Ko Mak
Ko Rang
Ban Hat Lek
Ko Kut
Phumĭ Thnál Krâbei
Kaôh Kŏng
f Thailand
50 km
31.1 mi

A
B
C
1
2
3
4
5
6
Kau-Ye K.
Hangapru
Forest Strait
Lampi K.
Karaturi
Clara I.
Sir Rob. Campbell I.
Wa-Ale K.
Lampi Island Marine Nat. Park
Khao Nam Noi
755
Pila K.
Pulo Buda
Nangin
Marang
Lord Loughborough I.
12
Heckford Bank
Investigator Channel
Maliwun
Zadetkale K.
Hastings I.
Macleod I.
Ulu
Kawthoung
Zadetkyi K.
Ranong
Andaman
Than K.
Ko Chang
950
Ko Pha Yam
Nam Sai
Christie I.
Kapoe
Laem Son N. P.
Ko Surin Nua
Mu Ko Surin
Mu Ko Surin Marine N. P.
Na Kha
Ko Surin Tai
139
1465
1406
Ko Ra
Si Phang-nga N. P.
Khuraburi
Sea
Ko Phra Thong
Khao Sok Nat. Park
Bang Wan
Ko Kho Khao
Ban Tak
Takua Pa
401
Tham Waram
Phanom
Khao Lak-Lam Ru N. P.
Bang Sak
Kapong
415
Ko Similan
Mu Ko Similan Marine N. P.
1048
Mu Ko Similan
Khao Lak Beach
Thap Put
Ko Payang
Khao Lam Pi - Hat Thai Muang N. P.
Phang Nga
Takua Thung
Thai Muang
Ao Luk
238
Laem Sak
Khok Kloi
Ao Phang-nga Marine N. P.
Than Bokkharani N.P.
Than Bok Khorani N. P.
129
Chat Chai
402
Sirinat Nat. P.
Ko Yao
Khao Phra Thaeo N. P.
Thalang
Ko Phuket
Kathu
Ko Yao Yai
Hat Patong
Beach
Thap Tai
546
Phuket
Hat Karon
Ko Phi Phi Don
Ko Phi Phi Le
50 km
31.1 mi
Ko Racha Yai
Ko Racha Noi

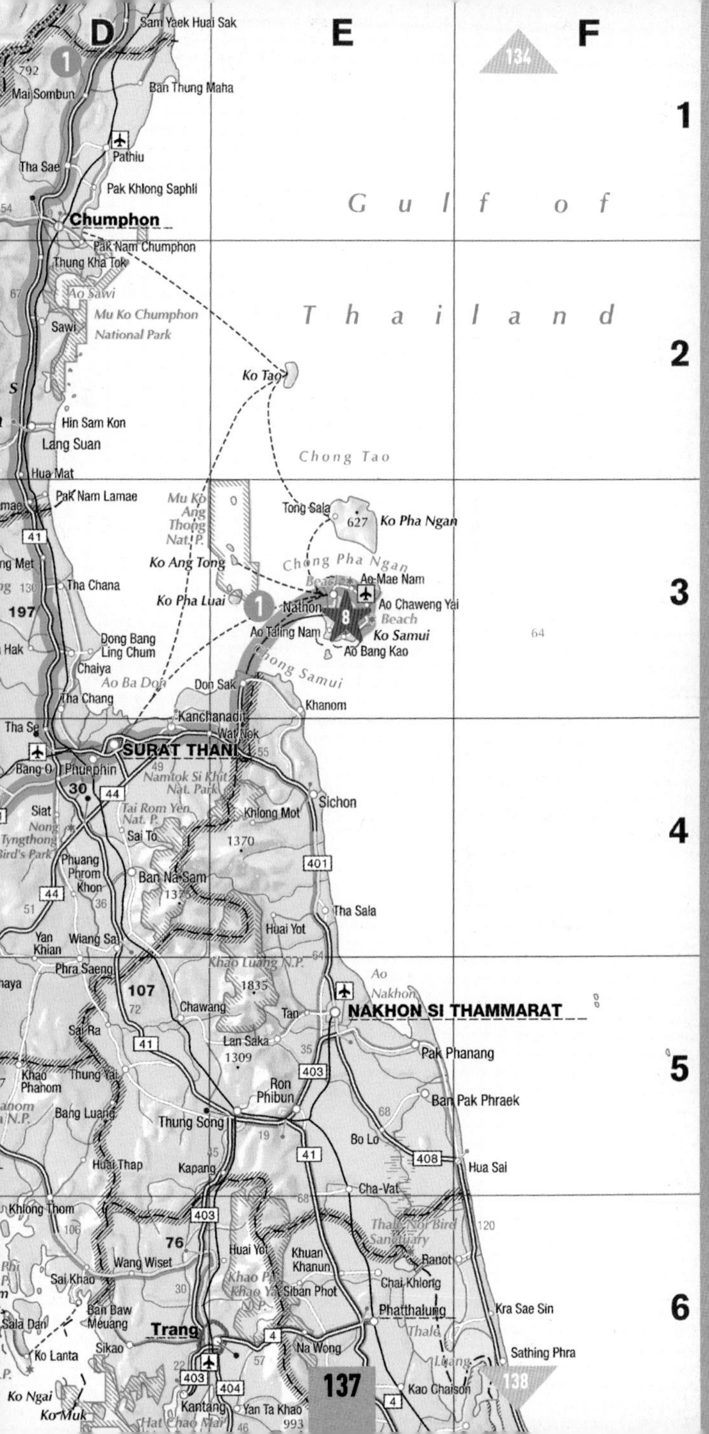
D
E
F
134
1
2
3
4
5
6
Sam Yaek Huai Sak
Mai Sombun
Ban Thung Maha
Pathiu
Tha Sae
Pak Khlong Saphli
Chumphon
Pak Nam Chumphon
Thung Kha Tok
Ao Sawi
Mu Ko Chumphon National Park
Sawi
Gulf of Thailand
Ko Tao
Hin Sam Kon
Lang Suan
Hua Mat
Chong Tao
Pak Nam Lamae
Mu Ko Ang Thong Nat. P.
Tong Sala
Ko Pha Ngan
Ko Ang Tong
Chong Pha Ngan
Ao Mae Nam
Tha Chana
Ko Pha Luai
Nathon
Ao Chaweng Yai Beach
Ao Taling Nam
Ko Samui
Ao Bang Kao
Dong Bang Ling Chum
Chaiya
Ao Ba Don
Chong Samui
Don Sak
Tha Chang
Khanom
Kanchanadit
Tha Se
Wat Nok
SURAT THANI
Bang O
Phunphin
Namtok Si Khit Nat. Park
Tai Rom Yen Nat. P.
Siat
Khlong Mot
Sichon
Nong Tyngthong Bird's Park
Sai To
Phuang Phrom Khon
Ban Na Sam
Tha Sala
Yan Khian
Wiang Sa
Huai Yot
Khao Luang N.P.
Phra Saeng
Ao Nakhon
Chawang
Tan
NAKHON SI THAMMARAT
Sai Ra
Lan Saka
Pak Phanang
Khao Phanom
Thung Yai
Ron Phibun
Bang Luang
Thung Song
Ban Pak Phraek
Bo Lo
Huai Thap
Kapang
Hua Sai
Cha-Vat
Khlong Thom
Thale Noi Bird Sanctuary
Huai Yot
Khuan Khanun
Ranot
Wang Wiset
Sai Khao
Khao Pu Khao Ya N.P.
Siban Phot
Chai Khlong
Ban Baw Meuang
Phatthalung
Kra Sae Sin
Sala Dan
Trang
Thale Luang
Na Wong
Ko Lanta
Sikao
Sathing Phra
Ko Ngai
Kantang
Yan Ta Khao
Kao Chaison
Ko Muk
Hat Chao Mai
138

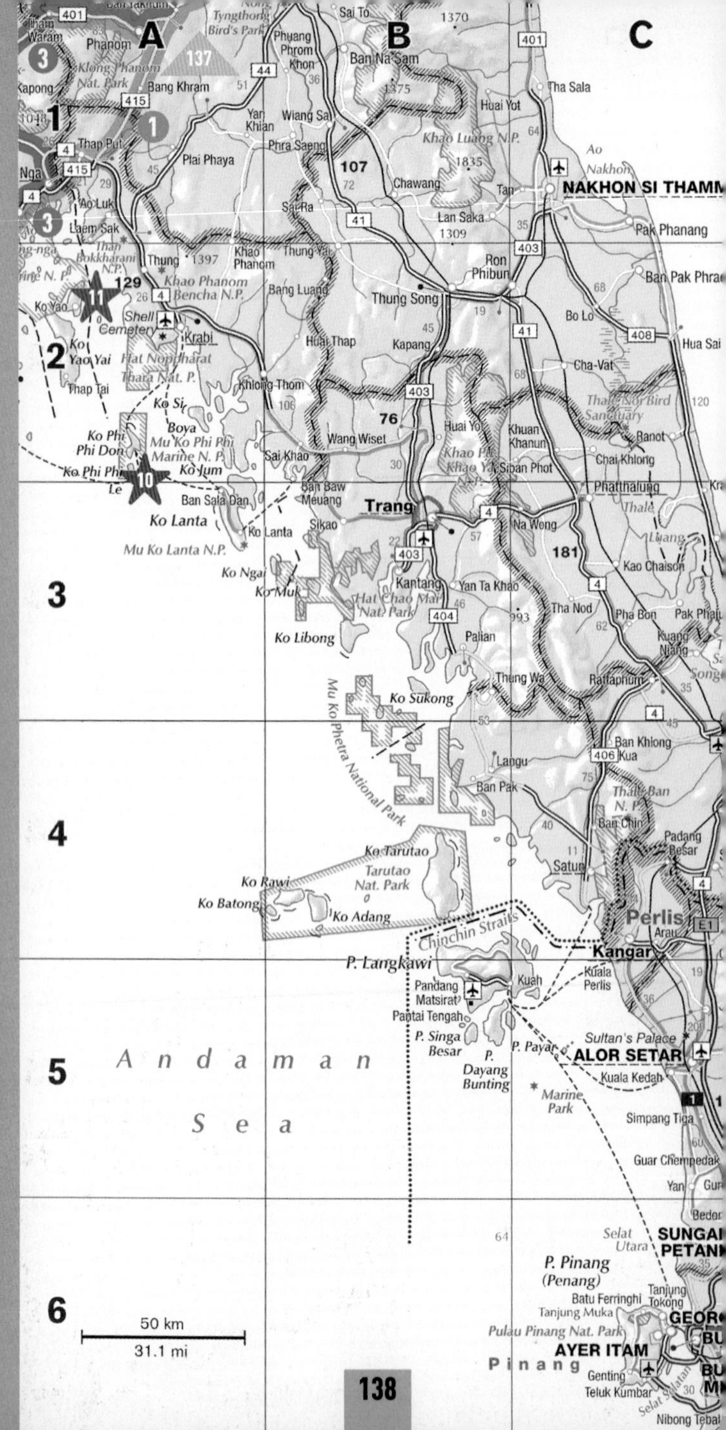
A
B
C
1
2
3
4
5
6
Phanom
Klong Phanom Nat. Park
Bang Khram
Tyngthong Bird's Park
Phuang Phrom Khon
Sai To
Ban Na Sam
Tha Sala
Huai Yot
Khao Luang N.P.
Yan Khian
Wiang Sa
Phra Saeng
Thap Put
Plai Phaya
Chawang
NAKHON SI THAMM
Ao Nakhon
Tan
Lan Saka
Sai Ra
Ao Luk
Laem Sak
Pak Phanang
Than Bokkharani N.P.
Thung
Khao Phanom
Thung Yai
Ron Phibun
Ban Pak Phra
Khao Phanom Bencha N.P.
Bang Luang
Thung Song
Bo Lo
Ko Yao
Shell Cemetery
Krabi
Ko Yao Yai
Hat Noppharat Thara Nat. P.
Thap Tai
Huai Thap
Kapang
Hua Sai
Cha-Vat
Khlong Thom
Thale Noi Bird Sanctuary
Ko Si Boya
Ko Phi Phi Don
Ko Phi Phi Le
Mu Ko Phi Phi Marine N.P.
Ko Jum
Wang Wiset
Huai Yot
Khuan Khanun
Ranot
Sai Khao
Khao Pu Khao Ya N.P.
Siban Phot
Chai Khlong
Phatthalung
Ban Sala Dan
Ko Lanta
Ban Baw Meuang
Trang
Sikao
Na Wong
Thale Luang
Mu Ko Lanta N.P.
Kao Chaison
Ko Ngai
Ko Muk
Kantang
Yan Ta Khao
Hat Chao Mai Nat. Park
Tha Nod
Pha Bon
Pak Phaju
Ko Libong
Palian
Kuang Niang
Thung Wa
Rattaphum
Ko Sukong
Mu Ko Phetra National Park
Ban Khlong
Kua
Langu
Ban Pak
Thale Ban N. P.
Ban Chin
Padang Besar
Ko Tarutao
Tarutao Nat. Park
Satun
Ko Rawi
Ko Batong
Ko Adang
Perlis
Arau
Chinchin Straits
Kangar
P. Langkawi
Kuah
Kuala Perlis
Pandang Matsirat
Pantai Tengah
P. Singa Besar
P. Dayang Bunting
P. Payar
Sultan's Palace
ALOR SETAR
Kuala Kedah
Marine Park
Andaman Sea
Simpang Tiga
Guar Chempedak
Yan
Selat Utara
SUNGAI PETANI
P. Pinang (Penang)
Batu Ferringhi
Tanjung Tokong
Tanjung Muka
Pulau Pinang Nat. Park
AYER ITAM
Pinang
Genting
Teluk Kumbar
Nibong Tebal
50 km
31.1 mi

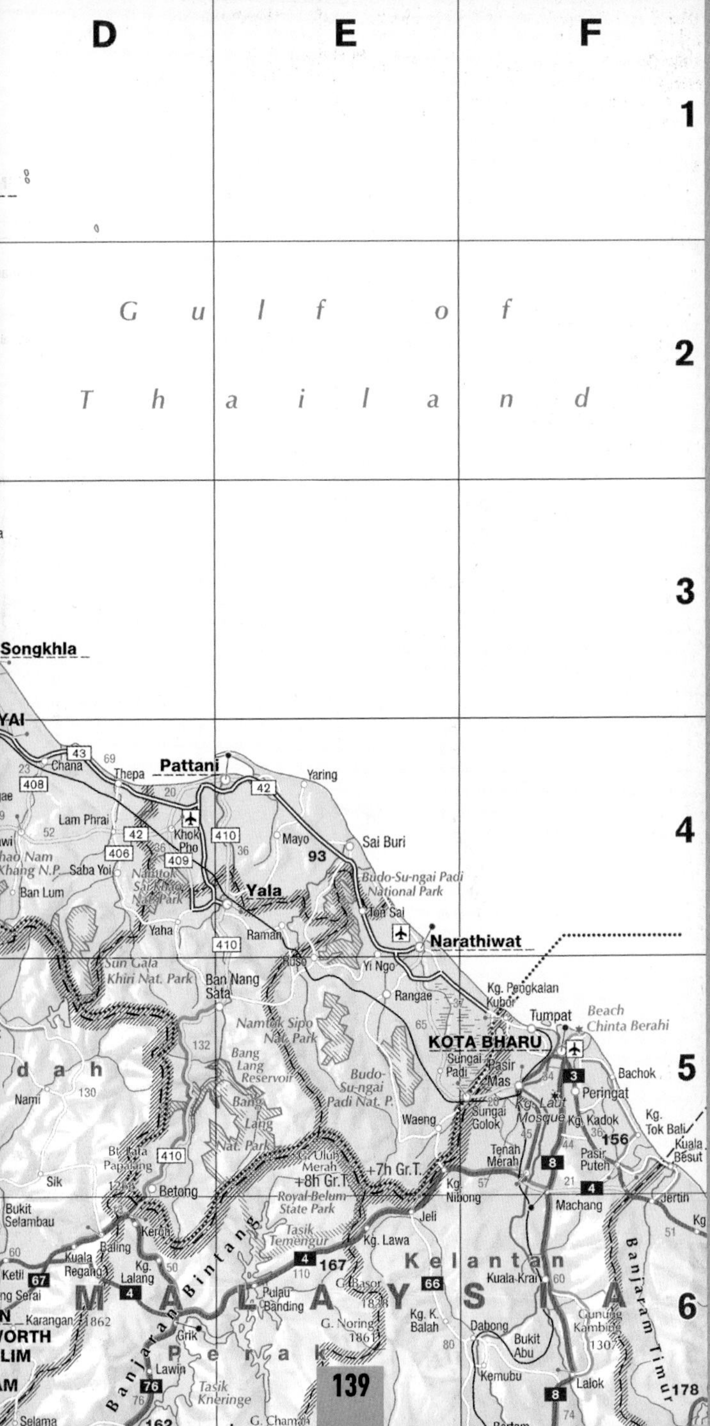
D
E
F
1
2
3
4
5
6
Gulf of Thailand
Songkhla
Pattani
Chana
Thepa
Yaring
Lam Phrai
Khok Pho
Mayo
Sai Buri
Saba Yoi
Ban Lum
Yala
Budo-Su-ngai Padi National Park
Ton Sai
Yaha
Raman
Narathiwat
Ruso
Yi Ngo
Sun Gala Khiri Nat. Park
Ban Nang Sata
Rangae
Kg. Pengkalan Kubor
Tumpat
Beach Chinta Berahi
KOTA BHARU
Sungai Padi
Pasir Mas
Bachok
Peringat
Kg. Laut Mosque
Kg. Kadok
Kg. Tok Bali
Kuala Besut
Sungai Golok
Waeng
Budo-Su-ngai Padi Nat. P.
Bang Lang Reservoir
Namtok Sipo Nat. Park
Tenah Merah
Pasir Puteh
Nami
Sik
Betong
+8h Gr.T.
+7h Gr.T.
Royal-Belum State Park
Kg. Nibong
Machang
Jertih
Jeli
Kg. Lawa
Bukit Selambau
Baling
Kuala Regang
Kg. Lalang
Banjaram Bintang
Kelantan
Kuala Krai
MALAYSIA
Pulau Banding
G. Basor 1838
G. Noring 1861
Kg. K. Balah
Dabong
Bukit Abu
Gunung Kambing 1307
Banjaram Timur
Grik
Perak
Lawin
Tasik Kneringe
Kemubu
Lalok
Selama
Karangan
1862
G. Chamah
Ketil
Tasik Temengur
Keroh

KEY TO ROAD ATLAS

Autobahn, mehrspurige Straße - in Bau Highway, multilane divided road - under construction		Autoroute, route à plusieurs voies - en construction Autosnelweg, weg met meer rijstroken - in aanleg
Fernverkehrsstraße - in Bau Trunk road - under construction		Route à grande circulation - en construction Weg voor interlokaal verkeer - in aanleg
Hauptstraße Principal highway		Route principale Hoofdweg
Nebenstraße Secondary road		Route secondaire Overige verharde wegen
Fahrweg, Piste Practicable road, track		Chemin carrossable, piste Weg, piste
Straßennummerierung Road numbering	E20 11 70 26 5 40 9	Numérotage des routes Wegnummering
Entfernungen in Kilometer Distances in kilometers	259 130 129	Distances en kilomètres Afstand in kilometers
Höhe in Meter - Pass Height in meters - Pass	1365	Altitude en mètres - Col Hoogte in meters - Pas
Eisenbahn - Eisenbahnfähre Railway - Railway ferry		Chemin de fer - Ferry-boat Spoorweg - Spoorpont
Autofähre - Schifffahrtslinie Car ferry - Shipping route		Bac autos - Ligne maritime Autoveer - Scheepvaartlijn
Wichtiger internationaler Flughafen - Flughafen Major international airport - Airport		Aéroport importante international - Aéroport Belangrijke internationale luchthaven - Luchthaven
Internationale Grenze - Provinzgrenze International boundary - Province boundary		Frontière internationale - Limite de Province Internationale grens - Provinciale grens
Unbestimmte Grenze Undefined boundary		Frontière d'Etat non définie Rijksgrens onbepaalt
Zeitzonengrenze Time zone boundary	-4h Greenwich Time -3h Greenwich Time	Limite de fuseau horaire Tijdzone-grens
Hauptstadt eines souveränen Staates National capital	MANILA	Capitale nationale Hoofdstad van een souvereine staat
Hauptstadt eines Bundesstaates Federal capital	Kuching	Capitale d'un état fédéral Hoofdstad van een deelstat
Sperrgebiet Restricted area		Zone interdite Verboden gebied
Nationalpark National park		Parc national Nationaal park
Antikes Baudenkmal Ancient monument		Monument antiques Antiek monument
Sehenswertes Kulturdenkmal Interesting cultural monument	Angkor Wat	Monument culturel interéssant Bezienswaardig cultuurmonument
Sehenswertes Naturdenkmal Interesting natural monument	Ha Long Bay	Monument naturel interéssant Bezienswaardig natuurmonument
Brunnen Well		Puits Bron
MARCO POLO Erlebnistour 1 MARCO POLO Discovery Tour 1		MARCO POLO Tour d'aventure 1 MARCO POLO Avontuurlijke Routes 1
MARCO POLO Erlebnistouren MARCO POLO Discovery Tours		MARCO POLO Tours d'aventure MARCO POLO Avontuurlijke Routes
MARCO POLO Highlight	1	MARCO POLO Highlight

FOR YOUR NEXT TRIP...

MARCO POLO TRAVEL GUIDES

Algarve
Amsterdam
Andalucia
Athens
Australia
Austria
Bali & Lombok
Bangkok
Barcelona
Berlin
Brazil
Bruges
Brussels
Budapest
Bulgaria
California
Cambodia
Canada East
Canada West / Rockies & Vancouver
Cape Town & Garden Route
Cape Verde
Channel Islands
Chicago & The Lakes
China
Cologne
Copenhagen
Corfu
Costa Blanca & Valencia
Costa Brava
Costa del Sol & Granada
Crete
Cuba
Cyprus (North and South)
Dresden
Dubai
Dublin
Dubrovnik & Dalmatian Coast
Edinburgh
Egypt
Egypt Red Sea Resorts
Finland
Florence
Florida
French Atlantic Coast
French Riviera (Nice, Cannes & Monaco)
Fuerteventura
Gran Canaria
Greece
Hamburg
Hong Kong & Macau
Iceland
India
India South
Ireland
Israel
Istanbul
Italy
Jordan
Kos
Krakow
Lake Garda
Lanzarote
Las Vegas
Lisbon
London
Los Angeles
Madeira & Porto Santo
Madrid
Mallorca
Malta & Gozo
Mauritius
Menorca
Milan
Montenegro
Morocco
Munich
Naples & Amalfi Coast
New York
New Zealand
Norway
Oslo
Paris
Phuket
Portugal
Prague
Rhodes
Rome
San Francisco
Sardinia
Scotland
Seychelles
Shanghai
Sicily
Singapore
South Africa
Sri Lanka
Stockholm
Switzerland
Tenerife
Thailand
Turkey
Turkey South Coast
Tuscany
United Arab Emirates
USA Southwest (Las Vegas, Colorado, New Mexico, Arizona & Utah)
Venice
Vienna
Vietnam
Zakynthos & Ithaca, Kefalonia, Lefkas

INDEX

This index contains all places, excursion destinations and beaches featured in this guide. Page numbers in bold type refer to the main entry..

WRITE TO US

e-mail: info@marcopologuides.co.uk

Did you have a great holiday?
Is there something on your mind?
Whatever it is, let us know!
Whether you want to praise, alert us to errors or give us a personal tip – MARCO POLO would be pleased to hear from you.
We do everything we can to provide the very latest information for your trip.

Nevertheless, despite all of our authors' thorough research, errors can creep in. MARCO POLO does not accept any liability for this. Please contact us by e-mail or post.

MARCO POLO Travel Publishing Ltd
Pinewood, Chineham Business Park
Crockford Lane, Chineham
Basingstoke, Hampshire RG24 8AL
United Kingdom

PICTURE CREDITS
Cover Photograph: young monks, Tempel Wat Phra Kaeo (Getty Images/ Axiom Photographic Agency: Acheson)
Images: DuMont Bildarchiv: Sasse (4 top., 26/27, 62); © fotolia.com: Mike Thomas (18 centre); Wilfried Hahn (34, 58, 99, 111); Getty Images/ Axiom Photographic Agency: Acheson (1); huber-images: Gräfenhain (4 bottom, 86), R. Leimer (48), F. Lukasseck (32/33), B. Morandi (46/47), Stadler (flap left), O. Stadler (2/3, 79), L. Vaccarella (29); huber-images/Picture Finder (115); © iStockphoto/jabejon (18 bottom); M. Kirchgessner (112); Laif/hemis.fr (61); Laif/Redux: Gräfenhain (89); K. Maeritz (68); mauritius images: Beck (113), Cassio (22), Vidier (8), Vidler (31), J. Warburton-Lee (107); mauritius images/Alamy (7, 9, 11, 18 o., 19 top, 28 left, 30, 30/31, 36/37, 38, 41, 52, 54, 56/57, 66, 70, 76, 84/85, 103, 114 bottom, 128/129), L. Duggleby (91); mauritius images/BlueHouse-Project (92/93); mauritius images/Imagebroker: J. Beck (72), D. Bleyer (50), S. Grassegger (19 bottom), K. Landwer-Johan (12/13), O. Stadler (64/65), M. Wolf (43); mauritius images/Imagebroker/GTW (44); mauritius images/McPHOTO (71); mauritius images/SuperStock (10); mauritus images/Alamy (6); mauritus images/Prisma (104/105); O. Stadler (flap right, 14/15, 20/21, 28 right, 74/75, 81, 82, 83, 112/113, 114 top); O. Stadler/A. Stubhan (25); T. Stankiewicz (17, 108/109); White Star: Reichelt (5)

2nd Edition – fully revised and updated 2016
Worldwide Distribution: Marco Polo Travel Publishing Ltd, Pinewood, Chineham Business Park, Crockford Lane, Basingstoke, Hampshire RG24 8AL, United Kingdom. Email: sales@marcopolouk.com

Chief editor: Marion Zorn
Author: Wilfried Hahn; co-author: Mischa Loose; editor: Felix Wolf
Programme supervision: Susanne Heimburger, Tamara Hub, Nikolai Michaelis, Kristin Schimpf, Martin Silbermann; picture editor: Gabriele Forst
What's hot: wunder media, Munich; Cartography road atlas: © MAIRDUMONT, Ostfildern
Cartography pull-out map: © MAIRDUMONT, Ostfildern
Design: milchhof : atelier, Berlin; Front cover, pull-out map cover, page 1: factor product munich; Discovery Tours: Susan Chaaban, Dipl.-Des. (FH)
Translated from German by M. Abdelhady, Bonn, Jennifer Walcoff Neuheiser, Tübingen; editor of the English edition: Tony Halliday, Oxford
Prepress: BW-Medien GmbH, Leonberg, writehouse, Cologne, InterMedia, Ratingen

Printed in China

DOS & DON'TS 

Some things are best avoided in Thailand

DISPLAYING ANGER

On rare occasions, the otherwise self-controlled Thai can become volatile, especially if alcohol is involved. Politely decline an invitation to a night out on the town by anyone you're not acquainted with, or simply excuse yourself after one drink. If you start to feel aggressive, stay calm. Also avoid inciting an already angry local to lose face.

INSULTING THE KING

Bhumibol Adulyadej claims that even he is not above reproach. Nevertheless, lese-majeste is liable to prosecution and can have serious repercussions, even for tourists. In 2009, Australian author Harry Nicolaides was sentenced to three years in prison for defaming the crown prince in his book. Although the king personally pardoned him, Nicolaides had to spend six months in a Thai prison.

NARCOTICS

Although Thailand carries the death penalty for drug trafficking, it is not unlikely that you will be offered some type of narcotic, for example, at the notorious full moon parties on Ko Phangan. But be careful: even the smallest trace of drugs such as *ganja* (marijuana) can end up sending you to prison!

MESSING AROUND WITH THE SCOOTER-MAFIA

Racing over the waves on a water scooter or jet ski might sound like innocent holiday fun, but there are some hidden dangers. Not only are these loud gas guzzlers a danger to swimmers and snorkelers, but also the locals who rent them out have a worse reputation than the so-called tuk-tuk mafia known for ripping off tourists. It is quite common for them to insist on a huge amount of money to compensate for supposed damages to the scooters, sometimes even with threats of violence.

SMUGGLERS

Smugglers lurk wherever there are tourists. They offer everything under the sun: gemstones, free sightseeing tours, prostitutes. As a rule, Thais act reserved around tourists and are not inclined to accost them on the street. If you are approached by a local, chances are you could be the target of a scam.

TRAVELLING IN THE DEEP SOUTH

Pattani, Yala and Narathiwat are the three southernmost provinces. The majority of the population is Muslim. Attacks in this region occur almost daily, and since 2004 an estimated 4,000 people have died as a result of the clashes. Terrorists want to force independence from Thailand. Avoid this crisis area!